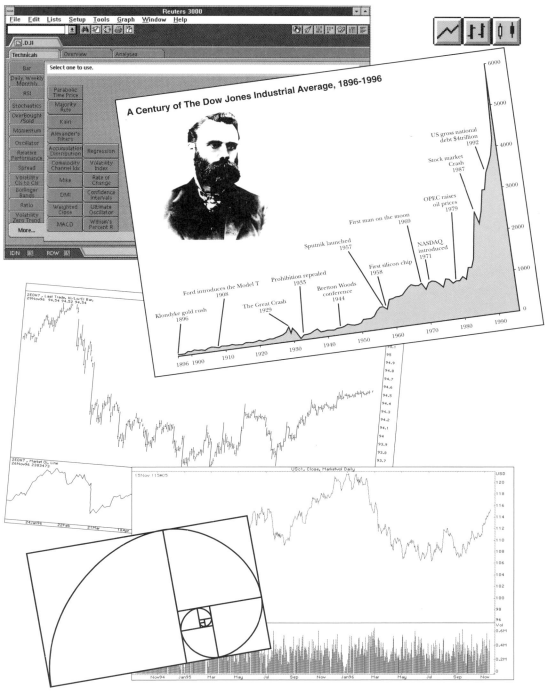

An Introduction to

Technical Analysis

John Wiley & Sons (Asia) Pte Ltd
Singapore   New York   Chichester
Brisbane   Toronto   Weinheim

Other titles in the series

An Introduction to Derivatives *0-471-83176-X*
An Introduction to Foreign Exchange & Money Markets *0-471-83128-X*
An Introduction to Equity Markets *0-471-83171-9*
An Introduction to Bond Markets *0-471-83174-3*
An Introduction to the Commodities, Energy & Transport Markets *0-471-83150-6*

You can get more information about the other titles in the series from the Reuters Financial Training series companion web site at *http://www.wiley-rft.reuters.com.*

Acknowledgments

The publishers and Reuters Limited would like to thank the following people for their invaluable assistance in this book:

Colin Nicholson of the Australian Technical Analysts Association for his thorough review of the book and constructive feedback.

Dr. Keith A. Rogers of Training and Learning Design who wrote, designed and produced the original version of the book.

Charles Kaplan, Presiden tof Equity Analytics Ltd, for permitting us to use his Glossary of Technical Analysis terms at the back of this book.

Haksu Kim of Pacific Investment Research, Inc., for the use of his Listing of Stock Markets Around the World at the back of this book.

Asoka Markandu, Tracy Khoo, Tay Liam Hwee and Michael Tarlinton of Reuters Asia Pte Ltd for their support and advice.

Thanks are also due to Dow Jones & Co. Inc. for supplying and giving permission to use the photograph of Charles Dow.

This publication is designed to provide accurate and authoritative information in
regard to the subject matter covered. It is sold with the understanding that the
publisher is not engaged in rendering professional services. If professional advice or
other expert assistance is required, the services of a competent professional person
should be sought.

Other Wiley Editorial Offices
John Wiley & Sons, Inc., 605 Third Avenue, New York, NY 10158-0012, USA
John Wiley & Sons Ltd, Baffins Lane, Chichester, West Sussex PO19
1UD, England
John Wiley & Sons (Canada) Ltd, 22 Worcester Road, Rexdale,
Ontario M9W 1L1, Canada
John Wiley & Sons (Australia) Ltd, 33 Park Road (PO Box 1226), Milton,
Queensland 4064, Australia
Wiley-VCH, Pappelallee 3, 69469 Weinheim, Germany

Library of Congress Cataloging-in-Publication Data
An introduction to technical analysis.
         p.   cm. — (The Reuters financial training series)
    Includes bibliographical references.
    ISBN 0-471-831271 (cloth)
    1. Investment Analysis.   2. Investment analysis — Charts, diagrams, etc.
    I. Series.
332.6 — dc21   98-42022
                                CIP

ISBN 0-471-83127-1

Typeset in 10/12 point New Baskerville
Printed in Singapore by Craft Print Pte Ltd
10 9 8 7 6 5 4

An Introduction to

Technical Analysis

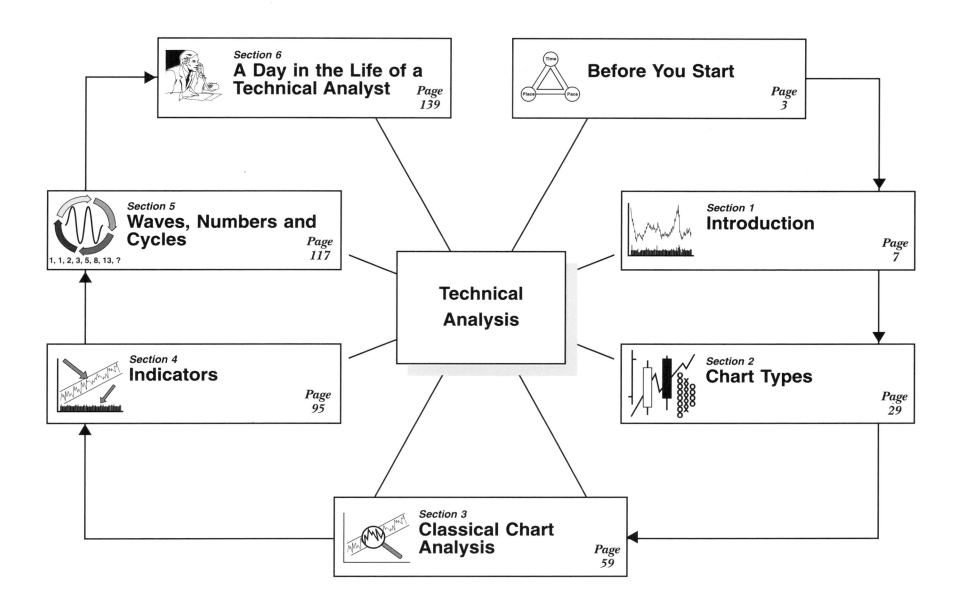

Contents

Who Should Use This Book?

This book is designed to provide an overview of technical analysis for a variety of readers: salespeople, support and operations staff, trainers, managers or the average investor who wants to learn how to use technical analysis in his own trading strategy. Also, anyone about to begin an in-depth study of technical analysis would find this book to be a useful primer. Technical analysis is a very complicated subject and the reader will be able to find volumes of information on the subject with which to continue studying.

Despite its complexity, technical analysis is no longer a tool only for investment experts. With the now common availability of historical price data via specialised electronic data sources, such as Reuters provides, or those sources available on the Internet to the public, technical analysis is a tool that can be used by all market players.

This book will take you through technical analysis from first principles, creating your first chart with pencil and paper, to being able to understand the concepts behind sophisticated analysis tools and techniques. By the time you have completed this book you will be able to use most of the main market techniques and understand when they should be applied.

You may also find this knowledge to be useful, as technical analysis is one of the subjects which forms part of the examination syllabus leading to either Fellowship or Associateship of the ACI Institute.

What Will You Find in This Book?

This book provides a new approach to gaining some basic familiarity with the essential concepts in the increasingly popular field of technical analysis. The book is written in a very accessible style with jargon kept to a minimum, but clearly explained when it is used.

Most importantly, the book includes a range of materials to help you reinforce what you are learning. Each section offers a solid explanation of basic concepts, followed by actual examples for the reader to work through. Additional exercises and quick quizzes enable the reader to further enhance learning. Finally, each chapter includes a graphic overview – a visual outline – of what has been covered for quick yet thorough review and ends with a listing of additional reference materials.

In addition, the **RFT Web Site** has been created as this series of books' companion web site where additional quiz questions, updated screens and other information may be found. You can find this web site at

http://www.wiley-rft.reuters.com.

How is This Book Organised?

This book contains the following sections:

Before You Start
This section!

Introduction
This summarises the development of technical analysis and the Dow Theory.

Chart Types
This section deals with the main ways in which prices and financial data can be plotted on a chart together with the uses for each chart type.

Classical Chart Analysis
Should I buy or sell? Charting techniques often give rise to patterns which can be used to help you decide.

Indicators
Can you predict future market trends? This section describes the various types of indicators available.

Waves, Numbers and Cycles
Markets follow cycles and patterns of buying and selling move in waves... or do they? Perhaps the markets are governed by mathematical laws or are they ruled by chaos?

A Day in the Life of a Technical Analyst
This is what it is really like!

Throughout the book you will find that important terms or concepts are shown in **bold**, for example, **Dow Theory**. You will also find that activities included to enhance your learning are indicated by the following icons:

This indicates the definition of a term that you must know and understand to master the material.

This means stop and think about the point being made. You may also want to jot a few words in the box provided.

This indicates an activity for you to do. It is usually something written – for example, a definition, notes, or a calculation.

This is the answer or response to an activity and it usually follows the activity or is close to it.

This indicates the main points of the section.

This indicates questions for you to answer to help you to review the material. The answers are also provided.

This indicates the one-page summary that provides a quick overview of the entire section. This page serves as an excellent study tool.

Additional reference material is listed in **Further Resources** at the end of each section.

How to Use This Book

Before you start using this book, decide what you want from the material. If you are using it as part of your work, discuss with your manager how he/she will help by giving time for study and giving you feedback and support. Although your learning style is unique to you, you will find that your learning is much more effective if you allocate reasonable sized periods of time for study. The most effective learning period is about 30 minutes – so use this as a basis. If you try to fit your learning into odd moments in a busy schedule you will not get the best from the materials or yourself. You might like to schedule learning periods into your day just as you would business meetings.

Remember that the most effective learning is an interactive process and requires more than just reading the text. The exercises in this book make you think through the material you have just read and then apply your understanding through basic activities. Take time to do the exercises. This old Chinese saying sums up this concept:

> **I hear and I forget**
> **I see and I remember**
> **I do and I understand**

Try to make sure your study is uninterrupted. This probably means that your workplace is not a good environment! You will need to find both the time and place where you can study – you may have access to a quiet room at work, you may have a room at home, you may need to use a library.

It's important to remember that learning is not a race – everyone learns at their own rate. Some people find things easy, some not quite so easy. So don't rush your learning – make sure you get the most from the book.

Remember it's your learning – so it's up to you.

This section of the book should take no more than 60 minutes of study time. You may not take as long as this or you may take a little longer – remember your learning is individual to you.

'He was an experienced newspaper reporter, with an early training under Samuel Bowles, the great editor of the Springfield Republican. Dow was a New Englander, intelligent, self-repressed, ultra-conservative, and he knew his business... Knowing and liking Dow, with whom I worked in the last years of his life, I was often, with many of his friends, exasperated by his conservatism... In the language of the prize ring, he pulled his punches.'

How Good is the Dow Theory? Part 1 by Bill Dunbar
Technical Analysis of Stocks and Commodities , Vol. 3:2 (59-63), 1985

What is Market Analysis?

Since the early days of buying and selling shares and trading in such commodities as rice, traders and investors have noted trends and patterns in their prices over time. Modern markets abound in sayings such as:

> *The trend is your friend*
>
> *Go with the trend*

But what do these phrases really mean? And what is the value of using charts, such as the one shown below of the Dow Jones Industrial Average, which can be seen in such financial publications as the *Financial Times* and *The Wall Street Journal*, and on electronic data systems.

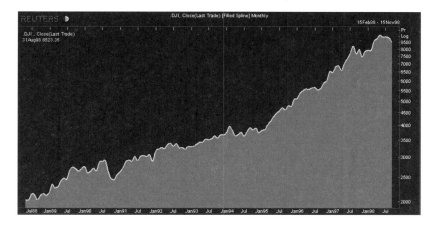

You may have asked yourself questions such as:

- Where did these sayings originate?
- Are these sayings true and what use are they?
- Who uses these charts?
- What do these charts indicate?

Most individual and institutional investors, traders, brokers, dealers and other market participants are seeking the best return on their investments or best profit on their deals. It is obvious then that they will welcome any method they can employ to reduce their risk of losing money and improve their chance of reaping rewards. But is it possible to identify when is a good time to buy or sell shares, trade futures contracts, etc?

Market players use charts and analytical tools to identify changes in supply and demand for traded financial instruments, which helps them to forecast prices and formulate trading strategies for all financial markets. Some of the more familiar chart uses involve the following:

- Whole stock markets (market indices)
- Stock market sectors (sector indices)
- Individual shares
- Currencies
- Interest rates (bonds, bills, treasury notes, etc.)
- Commodities (agriculturals, metals, energy and softs)
- Futures
- Options

There are two basic types of market analysis available to guide market players, each having its own experts:

- **Fundamental analysis**

- **Technical analysis or charting**

In practice, most investors and traders adopt tools and techniques from both types of analysis.

Fundamental Analysis

Fundamental analysis may be defined as follows:

Fundamental analysis is a method of forecasting the future price movements of a financial instrument based on economic, political, environmental and other relevant factors and statistics that will affect the basic supply and demand of whatever underlies the financial instrument.

The fundamental analyst identifies and measures factors that determine the intrinsic value of a financial instrument, such as the general economic and political environment, and including any that affect supply and demand for the underlying product or service. If there is an increase in supply but the level of demand remains the same, then there will be an increase in market prices. An increase in supply produces the opposite effect.

For example, an analyst for a listed company studies the supply and demand for the company's products or services; its management quality and policies; its historic and forecasted performance; its future plans, prospects and the plans of its competitors; industry statistics; general economic conditions; and government policy. A commodity analyst studies the commodity's statistics of price, supply, demand and inventory levels; forecasts of usage; planned production or planting; weather forecasts and conditions; availability of substitutes; economic conditions; and political developments.

From this data, the analyst constructs a model to determine the instrument's current and forecasted value. The basic idea is that unmatched increases in supply tend to depress prices, while unmatched increases in demand tend to increase prices. Once the analyst estimates intrinsic value, he compares it to current prices and decides whether prices ought to rise or fall. The basic premise is: If price is currently less than value, then price should rise. If price is currently above value, then price should fall.

One difficulty with fundamental analysis is accurately measuring the relationships among the variables. Necessarily, the analyst must make estimates based on experience. In addition, the markets tend to anticipate events and discount them in price in advance. Finally, serving as both a disadvantage and even as an advantage (depending upon the timing), the markets often take time to recognise that prices are out of line with value.

Technical Analysis

Technical analysis may be defined as follows:

Technical analysis is a method of predicting price movements and future market trends by studying charts of past market action which take into account price of instruments, volume of trading and, where applicable, open interest in the instruments.

Technical analysis is concerned with what has *actually* happened in the market, rather than what should happen. A technical analyst will study the price and volume movements of a financial instrument and from that data create charts - again, derived from the actions of the market players - to use as his primary tool. The technical analyst is not much concerned with any of the "bigger picture" factors affecting the market, as is the fundamental analyst, but concentrates on the activity of that instrument's market.

Therefore, technical analysis is also a subjective "art" or skill whose success depends a great deal on the analyst's experience. Even experienced analysts will at times disagree on the interpretation of a chart. For example, two analysts might disagree on the definition of a timeframe, with one analyst believing a price is likely to rise in the short term, while the other sees this as no more than a rally in a longer term downward trend. So why is technical analysis so important in the market place?

The Underlying Principles of Technical Analysis

Technical analysis is based on three underlying principles:

1. **Market action discounts everything**	This means that the actual price is a reflection of everything that is known to the market that could affect it, for example, supply and demand, political factors and market sentiment. The pure technical analyst is only concerned with price movements, not with the reasons for any changes.
2. **Patterns exist**	Technical analysis is used to identify patterns of market behaviour which have long been recognised as significant. For many given patterns there is a high probability that they will produce the expected results. Also there are recognised patterns which repeat themselves on a consistent basis.
3. **History repeats itself**	Chart patterns have been recognised and categorised for over 100 years and the manner in which many patterns are repeated leads to the conclusion that human psychology changes little with time.

If all the above principles were valid, then technical analysis would be closer to a science than an art. The reality is that history does not always repeat itself exactly and patterns do not always occur exactly as before. The result is that technical analysis is a subjective skill, with the interpretation of charts and market behaviour forecasting dependent on the skills of individual analyst. The future cannot be predicted necessarily, with certainty, from past events. Technical analysts consider the probability that a given situation will produce a given result and in some cases, this probability is very high.

Technical v Fundamental Analysis

The following table broadly summarises the differences between the two types of analysis:

Fundamental Analysis	Technical Analysis

• Focuses on what *ought* to happen in a market
• Factors involved in price analysis include:
 	
  • Supply and demand
  • Seasonal cycles
  • Weather
  • Government policy
	• Focuses on what *actually* happens in a market
	• Charts are based on market action involving:
	
	  • Price
	  • Volume – all markets
	  • Open interest – futures only

In practice, many market players use technical analysis in conjunction with fundamental analysis to determine their trading strategy. One major advantage of technical analysis is that experienced analysts can follow many markets and market instruments, whereas the fundamental analyst needs to know a particular market intimately.

Technical Analysis for Different Markets

The first known recording of prices and their subsequent analysis is attributed to **Munehisa Honma**, the inventor of Japanese candlesticks, in the early 1700s. However, most analysts consider the charting principles developed by Charles H Dow in the late 1800s and set out in his newspaper editorials of 1900 to 1902 to be the genesis of technical analysis. Dow was a member of the New York Stock Exchange and applied his techniques to the US stock market. He was the same man who subsequently established the Dow Jones news service and *The Wall Street Journal*.

Introduction

Technical analysis concepts are now applied to a wide range of shares, stock indices, interest rates, foreign exchange and derivatives contracts. Although the basic techniques are the same in all markets there are some important differences between two of the more important markets dealing with shares and derivatives. Highlights of these differences are summarised in the table below:

Factor	Equities	Derivatives
Instrument Life Span	Stocks and shares do not generally have expiry dates like derivative instruments. They remain trading unless the company or trust fails in some way, or is taken over. Exceptions are options, warrants, contributing and installment issues by companies, all of which have expiry dates.	Most commodities futures contracts are short-term with 3 month expiry dates. This means any charting can only be for a short term. Some charts are produced for hourly price changes. However, using continuation charts, produced by joining/splicing data for consecutive periods, means that the contracts can be charted over a longer period than each individual contract's life.
Adjustments	A great number of adjustments to equity prices may be required to ensure the data stream is comparable over time. Adjustments must be made for issues of additional equity, splits, consolidations, capital repayments, payment of calls or installments and name changes.	Generally, adjustments are not necessary to derivatives, other than some equity derivatives. However, the short life of futures contracts means that long-term studies require the artificial creation of what is called a "continuous contract." This is a notional joining together of the data streams for consecutive contracts. Several methods are used, none of which is ideal.

Factor	Equities	Derivatives
Trading Period	This is less of a problem for stocks and shares, because they tend to trade, with any liquidity, on one main market, which is used for most analysis purposes.	Derivative markets are increasingly being traded on more than one market, usually in different time zones. Even within the same market, trading continues on computerised markets after-hours. This poses real conceptual problems for methods based on a period (like bar charting), when the market does not have clearly defined trading sessions. Some markets, like currencies, never really close but trade continuously around the globe, one market taking over as a previous time zone closes.
Pricing Structure	Within the same stock market, prices are quoted in the same monetary units. However, there is an increasing tendency for companies to trade on several markets, usually in different currencies and sometimes in different configurations (eg, depository receipts of multiple share parcels).	Commodity futures contracts can have different specifications for the same commodity, as well as trade in different currencies, making comparison very difficult. Financial futures have these same problems and in addition, will have a value derived from a different underlying financial instrument. Where the financial future is based on an equity market index, there may be more than one index for a given market, both with different derivative contracts or traded on different markets.

Factor	Equities	Derivatives
Leverage	Equity markets tend to be traded without leverage, but this is by no means universal. Company-issued options and warrants should be considered as leveraged instruments, except that there may be no margin calls if they lose value, simply expiring worthless.	All derivative markets are highly leveraged. Small price movements can generate large profits and losses. Unrealised losses need to be covered by margin calls. Derivative markets tend to be traded more short-term, except for commercial hedging positions in the physical commodity or instrument. They also tend to be driven more by psychology —fear and greed primarily.
Short Selling	Equity markets tend to be traded primarily from the long side, with hedging and speculative short positions taken through derivatives; however, this is not common to all markets. Some markets allow easy shorting of equities, while others make it relatively complicated and difficult in various markets.	In all derivative markets, it is equally simple to trade from either the long or the short side. This increases the possibility of profits, makes for greater liquidity and tends to increase volatility.

Factor	Equities	Derivatives
Quality of Data	The data supplied from computerised markets is excellent in terms of both speed and accuracy; however, in non-computerised markets, both speed and accuracy are a problem. Recording volume is a particular difficulty, with quite different methodologies used in various markets.	As with equities, data from computerised markets is excellent. However, most futures markets are yet to be fully computerised, throwing real doubt on the accuracy of data and certainly making short-term trading difficult without direct access to the trading floor. In most markets, accurate volume and open interest is not available until the next day. There are also methodology differences between markets in the way open interest is calculated, that greatly complicates analysis.

The Strengths and Weaknesses of Technical Analysis

The following table broadly summarises the strengths and weaknesses of technical analysis.

Strengths	Weaknesses
• Technical analysis can be used to follow a wide range of instruments in almost any market place. • Charts can be used to analyse data for time periods ranging from hours to a century – the Dow Jones Industrial Average has been in constant use since May 26th, 1896. • There are many technical analysis tools and techniques available which have been developed to cater to the needs of different market sectors. • The basic principles of technical analysis are easy to understand and have been developed from the way markets operate – technical analysis is concerned with what is *actually* happening in markets. • Technical analysis relies on the use of accurate and timely data, which is available real-time or with only a short time delay when necessary.	• Because technical analysis has an element of subjectivity, it is possible for even experienced analysts to disagree on what data means and it is easy for undisciplined analysts to see what they want to see in a chart or to choose evidence selectively. Nor are technical analysts immune from the human tendency to become emotionally attached to predictions. • Technical analysis is based on the idea that human nature is constant and therefore that patterns tend to repeat themselves; however, there are limits to the extent to which the future can be simply extrapolated from the past. • Technical analysis is concerned with the degree of probability that an event will happen – not the certainty of the event. • Some modern technical analysis techniques are based on quite complex mathematical and statistical concepts. Computerised analysis software has largely overcome the difficulties of calculation, but understanding the output and applying it correctly is not easy. • It is vital for the success of technical analysis that the information used is both accurate and timely.

Whatever its weaknesses, technical analysis is now firmly established as an analytical tool and is practised and used by a growing number of market players for many reasons including:

- An increased market awareness of the success of technical analysis techniques

- An increased need for short-term trading, for which fundamental analysis, with infrequent and lagged data sources, is unsuitable

- The ever-increasing power, falling costs and availability of personal computers and sophisticated technical analysis software

- A growing realisation that fundamental analysis is poor on timing and that technical analysis can add value in this area

Trading Theories, Market Players and Analysis

There is a vast amount of data and a wide range of analytical techniques now available to help market players choose what instruments to invest in and when to do so. How individuals select their trading theory or strategy depends much on the market in which individual market players operate. A few years ago a futures trader, Grant D Noble, suggested that there were three theories of trading which highlighted different market players and their use of technical and fundamental analysis. Although some of the terms used for each theory may be unfamiliar now, by the time you finish this book you will have covered most of them. If you compare the contents of the book with this practitioner's view you will see there is little difference – just the way the techniques are combined.

It is worth noting that this is one market expert's definition of how to define the categories of technical analysis theory. Not all technical analysts would subscribe to the same categories.

Theory A – Market Equilibrium

- **Indicators** – Oscillators, eg, Relative Strength Index (RSI)

- **Number theory** – Fibonacci numbers, Gann numbers

- **Waves** – Elliott Wave Theory

- **Gaps** – High/Low, Open/Closing

Favoured by experts

Theory B – Classical Technical Analysis

- **Trends** – following Moving averages, etc

- **Chart formations** – Triangles, Head & Shoulders etc

- **Trend lines** – Channels

- **Cycles**

Favoured by public advisors

Theory C – Supply and Demand Fundamentals

- **Spreads** – Months, Exchanges, Cash/futures

- **Flow of funds** – Volume and open interest

- **Seasonals** – Weather, economy

- **Reports** – Expectations versus reality

Favoured by floor traders

Whichever type of market player you are interested in will influence the way you use this book. However, all the factors involved in the above theories have either been mentioned already or are discussed later.

Having reviewed the various theories in the previous section, you may find it useful before moving on to note here any technical analysis techniques and their application to a market sector that particularly interests you. For example, if you are interested in buying and selling shares, which techniques would you like to know more about?

Producing a Chart

This book is designed to give you the basic knowledge and understanding of the principles and techniques used in technical analysis and the various tools available to assist in technical analysis.

Before moving on to learn about the more detailed aspects of technical analysis, try the following activity.

Producing a Chart: Exercise 1
The data opposite shows the closing prices for Reuters shares over a 50-day period in early 1996.

All you need to do on the graph paper on the opposite page is mark the closing price on the vertical axis for each day. Use a pencil to mark each price with a cross or dot – any mistakes can easily be erased. Then join your marks to produce your chart – you may find using a color helps.

Although many computer graphing or technical analysis programs will produce the same results, by carrying out this exercise you will see how straightforward charting can be at a basic level. You will produce the simplest form of a chart that connects consecutive closing prices for an instrument – it is called a **line chart**.

Once you have drawn your chart, look closely to see if you can find any patterns. If you can, indicate them on your chart.

The chart of what you should see is shown on page 16.

1	766.5	26	797
2	770	27	784
3	769	28	789
4	758	29	789
5	751	30	779
6	749	31	778
7	753.5	32	770
8	777	33	765
9	794	34	765
10	782	35	756
11	764	36	750.5
12	771	37	747
13	773	38	755
14	773	39	751.5
15	761	40	756
16	752	41	746
17	758	42	746
18	750	43	756
19	743	44	762
20	745	45	777
21	747	46	781
22	764	47	777
23	789	48	767
24	780	49	767
25	792	50	760.5

* *The Reuters share data above is from the London market and is expressed in GB (Great British) pence sterling. The market trades in pence and tenths of a penny.*

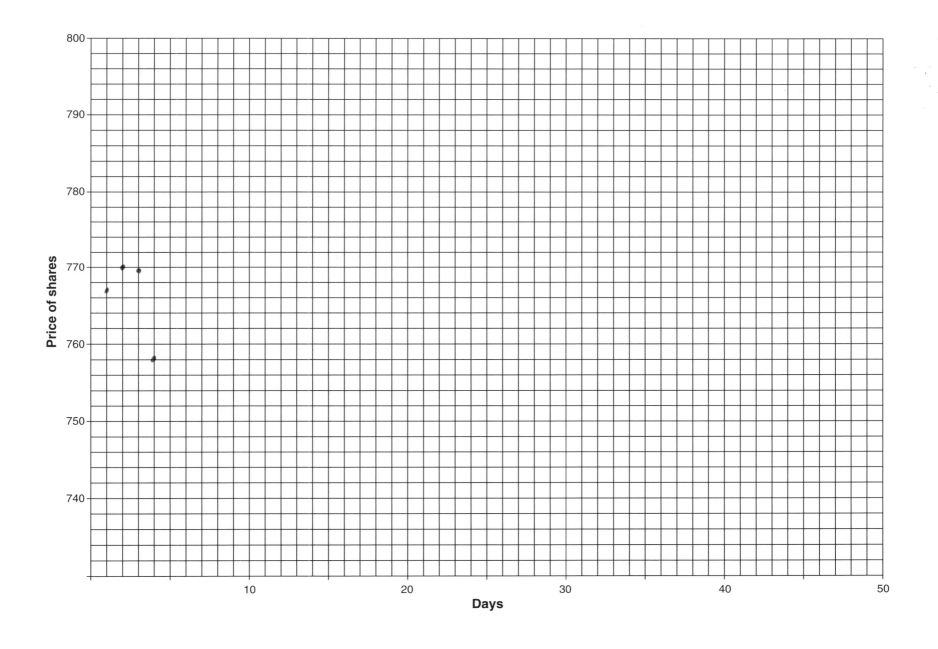

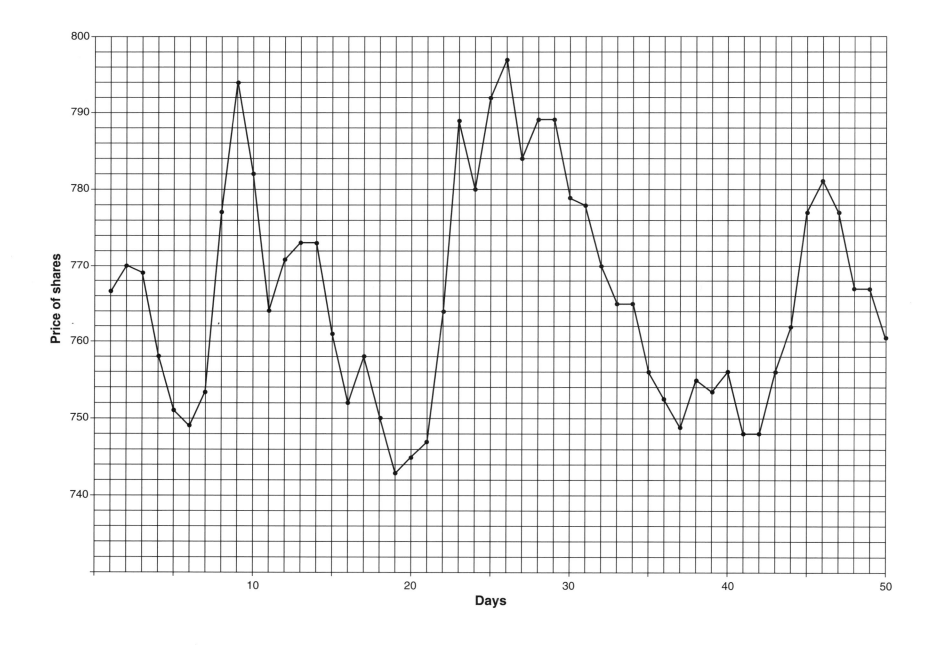

Producing a Chart: Exercise 1
You should have produced a chart similar to that shown on the previous page.

Having drawn the chart, which should not have been too difficult, you may have seen these patterns:

① A pattern showing a downward trend in the prices from day 10 to 19

② The pattern between day 22 and 30 resembles a head and shoulders of a person

③ On either side of day 40 is a "double bottom"

④ A large trading range is forming for this stock (ie, 742 to 798) over a short-term period

Looking at this chart, if an investor had bought shares on day 21 at 747 and sold them on day 31 at 770, then his or her profit — excluding any brokerage fees — would have been 23p per share.

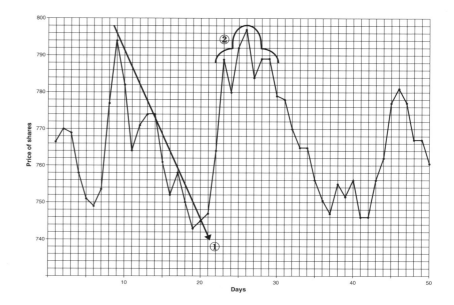

You have now produced your first chart! The exercise should not have been very demanding and from your results you can probably appreciate what practical use charting can be put to in a very simple way. However, market players will be basing their trading strategies on a little more than a line chart over 50 days for any particular share!

Dow Theory – The Genesis of Technical Analysis

Charles Henry Dow

The origins of modern technical analysis can be traced back to the work and theories of Charles Henry Dow (1851 – 1902). As a young man, Dow arrived in New York in 1879 to be a reporter for a financial news service. By 1882 he and Edward D Jones had founded *Dow Jones and Company* and were delivering their own news items to Wall Street financial houses.

By studying the closing prices of shares Dow concluded that it was possible to produce a market 'barometer' or **stock** average that could be used by investors to measure the **overall** performance of the stock market. In July 1884, Dow produced his first market measure calculated from the average of eleven stocks. This was called the **Railroad Average** because nine of the stocks were railroad companies. This first stock average was published intermittently in his company's *Customer's Afternoon Letter,* which was the forerunner of *The Wall Street Journal,* first published in 1889.

Along with his financial publishing interests, Dow was also a member of the New York Stock Exchange between 1885 and 1891. Dow continued to study the market data and by 1896 he had decided that his original index presented only a partial picture of the economy. Dow had concluded that two separate measures of the economy would provide confirmation of any broad market trend. So he introduced the **Industrial Average**, which was the average closing price of 12 stocks of what were then considered to be highly speculative, industrial companies.

The **Dow Jones Industrial Average** was first published on May 26th, 1896 in *The Wall Street Journal.* Along with the Railroad Average, now known as the Transportation Average, these indices have been published in every issue of *The Wall Street Journal* ever since.

The original 12 companies in the Industrial Average were expanded to 30 in 1928 and remain at this number today. Only one company remains in the average under its original name – the General Electric Company. The composition of the companies used to calculate the average changes from time to time to reflect changes in the economy and maintain its broad market representation.

The first day average close was 40.94, which was almost repeated again in 1932 during the depths of the US Depression. It took until 1972 for the average to reach 1000 but only a few years to rise from 4000 to over 5500 – its current level in 1996. The present day value is some 140 times its original value, but the Dow Jones Industrial Average is still seen as a popular barometer of the US stock market.

The chart opposite shows the fortunes of the Dow Jones Industrial Average over the past 100 years, together with some important historical events.

The Original Dow 12

American Cotton Oil
American Sugar Refining Co.
American Tobacco
Chicago Gas
Distilling & Cattle Feeding Co.
General Electric Co.
Laclede Gas Light Co.
National Lead
North American Co.
Tennessee Coal, Iron & Railroad Co.
US Leather
US Rubber Co.

A Century of the Dow Jones Industrial Average, 1896 - 1996

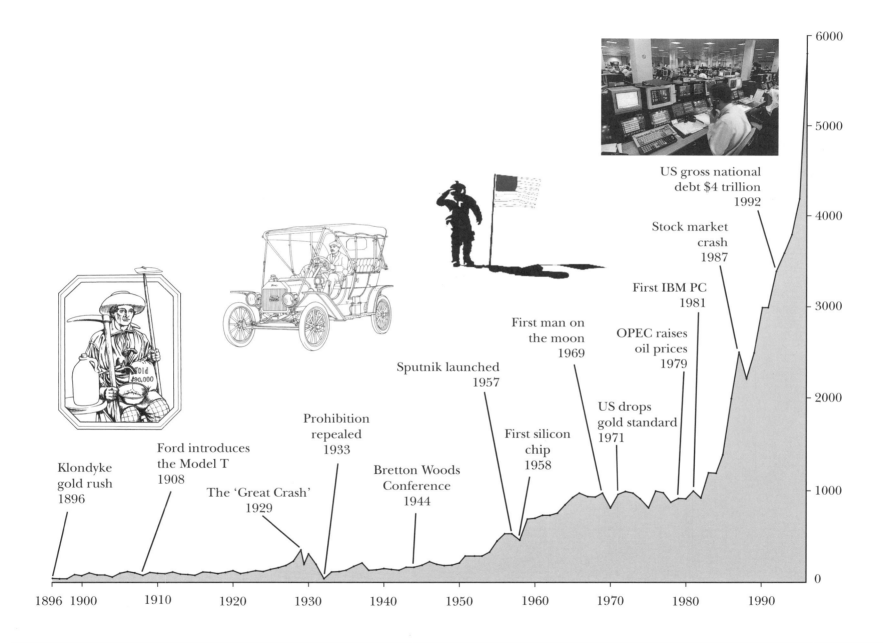

Klondyke
gold rush
1896

Ford introduces
the Model T
1908

The 'Great Crash'
1929

Prohibition
repealed
1933

Bretton Woods
Conference
1944

Sputnik launched
1957

First silicon
chip
1958

First man on
the moon
1969

US drops
gold standard
1971

OPEC raises
oil prices
1979

First IBM PC
1981

Stock market
crash
1987

US gross national
debt $4 trillion
1992

Introduction

As has already been mentioned, Dow was a member of the New York Stock Exchange and in his continuing studies of the markets he formulated what is now known as **Dow Theory**.

Dow never wrote a book about his theories but he published them as a series of *Wall Street Journal* editorials around the turn of the century. These editorials were collected together and reprinted in 1903, a short time after Dow's death in December 1902.

Dow had noted that a simple line plot of average price against time gave rise to zig-zag patterns which defined market **trends**. It is these basic patterns which technical analysts still use today, albeit with many refinements.

Dow formulated **six basic principles** from his study of the markets, which are summarised as follows:

1. **Average prices discount everything**

   Dow used **closing prices** exclusively to calculate his averages. He also assumed that the prices discounted everything – still an underlying assumption of technical analysis.

2. **The market moves in trends**

   Uptrends have a pattern of rising peaks and troughs – downtrends have the opposite.

   Dow identified three distinct types of trend:

   - **Primary** or **major**. These lasted a year or more and could be considered to be like a **tide**.
   - **Secondary** or **intermediate**. These were like **waves** and lasted 3 weeks to 3 months.
   - **Minor**. These were like **ripples** and lasted for less than 3 weeks.

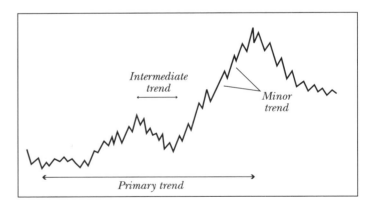

3. Major trends have three phases

Phase 1

This is an **accumulation** phase that moves sideways and during which astute investors are buying on an informed analytical basis.

Phase 2

This is an **uptrend** period where more investors begin to participate based on analysis and business news. Although the trend is up, the market prices zig-zag during **corrections** or **pullbacks**.

Phase 3

After a market price **peak** there is another accumulation period during which there is increased investor activity as the market news becomes more widely available.

The end of Phase 3 is marked by a downtrend and a return to a period of accumulation.

> *Ralph Nelson Elliott developed the Dow Theory further in the 1920s to provide an overall perspective of market movement expounded as **Elliott Wave Theory** – this is described later in Section 5.*

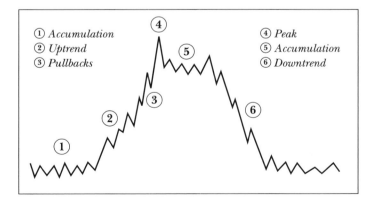

① *Accumulation*
② *Uptrend*
③ *Pullbacks*
④ *Peak*
⑤ *Accumulation*
⑥ *Downtrend*

4. Averages must confirm each other

Dow was convinced that both the Industrial and the Railroad averages had to be moving in the same direction to confirm a market trend.

> *These charts show modern Dow Jones averages – the upper charts show confirmation of the trend, while in the lower charts the markets are moving apart.*

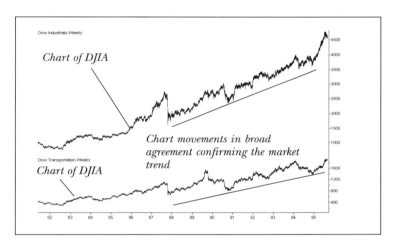

Chart of DJIA

Chart of DJIA

Chart movements in broad agreement confirming the market trend

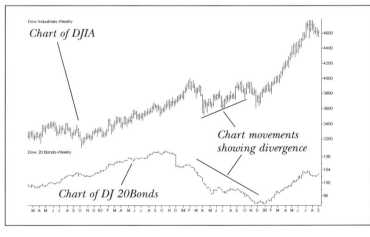

Chart of DJIA

Chart movements showing divergence

Chart of DJ 20Bonds

5. Volume must confirm the trend

Volume represents the total trading activity for a financial instrument in a particular time period. Dow considered volume to be important additional information in confirming market signals. The volume should expand in the direction of the major trend.

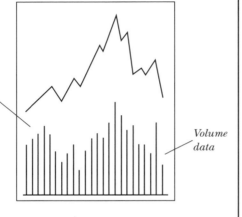

Confirmation when:
Increasing volume on uptrend highs and decreasing volume on uptrend lows – opposite for downtrend

Volume data

6. A trend is assumed to be in effect until it gives definite signals that it has reversed

This is the basis of trend analysis but it is not always easy to identify a trend reversal. For example, is a change just a correction or the start of a down- trend?

Modern technical analysts have a number of tools and techniques available to help which are described later:

• Support and resistance levels
• Trend lines
• Moving averages

Using Dow Theory Effectively

Dow's theories were never intended to indicate which specific stocks to buy or sell, but were intended to identify the stock market's major trend based on closing price information. Because this type of technical analysis is based on **trend-following**, it cannot predict exact beginnings and reversals of trends. Nor can charting the activity predict the exact duration and extent of trends. Despite these limitations, however, the Dow Theory has been used to give 40 correct signals in the period 1897 – 1991. During this period, only five incorrect signals were given.

Dow intended his averages to be market barometers, which meant that determining which individual stocks to buy or sell was entirely in the hands of investors. Originally, it was not possible to buy or sell a stock index, however, since the early 1980s, trading in stock index futures contracts has been possible. The Chicago Mercantile Exchange launched Standard & Poor 500 Stock Index futures in 1982 and LIFFE offered FT-SE 100 Stock Index futures and options in 1984.

Although Dow Theory has its limitations, it has provided the basis of many of the technical analysis techniques that are described later in this book.

Summary

You have now finished the first section of the book and you should have a clear understanding of:

- The differences between technical and fundamental analysis

- The underlying principles and uses of technical analysis

- The production of a basic chart

- The tenets of Dow Theory, which was the genesis of modern technical analysis

As a check on your understanding of this section, you should try the Quick Quiz Questions. You may also find the Overview section to be a helpful learning tool.

Quick Quiz Questions

1. Indicate "true" or "false" as to whether the following statements are underlying principles of technical analysis.

	True	False
a) The main focus is on what ought to happen in the market		
b) Patterns exist in market behaviour		
c) History repeats itself		
d) Market action discounts nothing		

2. According to Dow Theory, briefly describe what is happening in the various phases of a major trend numbered 1 to 6 in this diagram.

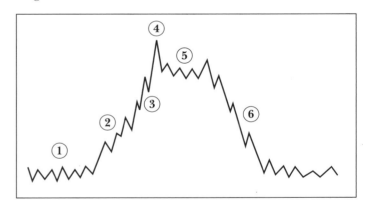

①

②

③

④

⑤

⑥

You can check your answers on page 26.

Overview

Technical v Fundamental Analysis

- Fundamental Analysis

  Fundamental analysis is a method of forecasting the future price movements of a financial instrument based on economic, political, environmental and other relevant factors and statistics that will affect the basic supply and demand of whatever underlies the financial instrument.

- Technical Analysis

  Technical analysis is a method of predicting price movements and future market trends by studying statistics of past market action which take into account price of instruments, volume of trading and, where applicable, open interest in the instruments.

- Summary of Differences

Fundamental Analysis	Technical Analysis
• Focuses on what *ought* to happen in a market	• Focuses on what *actually* happens in a market

• Factors involved in price analysis include:
  • Supply and demand
  • Seasonal cycles
  • Weather
  • Government policy
	• Charts are based on market action involving:
	  • Price
	  • Volume – all markets
	  • Open interest –
	    futures only

- Underlying Principles of Technical Analysis

1. Market action discounts everything	This means that the actual price is a reflection of everything that is known to the market that could affect it, for example, supply and demand, political factors and market sentiment. The pure technical analyst is only concerned with price movements, not with the reasons for any changes.
2. Patterns exist	Technical analysis is used to identify patterns of market behaviour which have long been recognised as significant. For many given patterns there is a high probability that they will produce the expected results. Also there are recognised patterns which repeat themselves on a consistent basis.
3. History repeats itself	Chart patterns have been recognised and categorised for over 100 years and the manner in which many patterns are repeated leads to the conclusion that human psychology changes little with time.

- Trading Theories

Theory A – Market Equilibrium

- **Indicators** – Oscillators, eg, Relative Strength Index (RSI)
- **Number theory** – Fibonacci numbers, Gann numbers
- **Waves** – Elliott Wave Theory
- **Gaps** – High/Low, Open/Closing

Favoured by experts

Theory B – Classical Technical Analysis

- **Trends** – following Moving averages, etc
- **Chart formations** – Triangles, Head & Shoulders etc
- **Trend lines** – Channels
- **Cycles**

Favoured by public advisors

Theory C – Supply and Demand Fundamentals

- **Spreads** – Months, Exchanges, Cash/futures
- **Flow of funds** – Volume and open interest
- **Seasonals** – Weather, economy
- **Reports** – Expectations versus reality

Favoured by floor traders

Introduction

The Genesis of Technical Analysis

❑ Charles Henry **Dow** first published the **Dow Jones Industrial Average** in *The Wall Street Journal* in 1896.

❑ Dow's **six basic principles**:
1. Average prices discount everything
2. The market moves in trends
3. Major trends have three phases
4. Averages must confirm each other
5. Volume must confirm the trend
6. A trend is assumed to be in effect until it gives definite signals that it has reversed

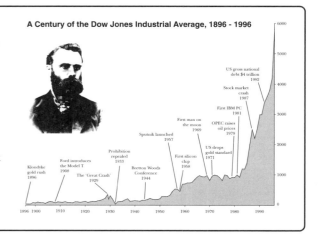

A Century of the Dow Jones Industrial Average, 1896 - 1996

Further Resources

Books

Technical Analysis of the Futures Markets
John J. Murphy, New York Institute of Finance, 1986
ISBN   0 13 898008 X

Technical Analysis Explained
Martin Pring, McGraw-Hill, 1991
ISBN   0 0705 1042 3

The New Commodity Trading Systems and Methods
Perry Kaufman, J. Wiley & Sons, 1987
ISBN   0 4718 7879 0

Technical Analysis from A – Z
Steven Achelis, Probus Publishing Co., 1995
ISBN   1 55738 816 4

Timing the Market – How to Profit in Bull and Bear Markets with Technical Analysis
Curtis M. Arnold, Probus Publishing Co., Revised Edition, 1993
ISBN   1 55738 496 7

Charters on Charting – How to Improve Your Stockmarket Decision Making
David Charters, Rushmere Wynne, 1995
ISBN   0 948035 21 8

The Futures Game
Richard J. Teweles and Frank J. Jones, McGraw-Hill Book Company, Second Edition
ISBN   0 07 063734 2

Schwager on Futures - Fundamental Analysis
Jack D. Schwager, J. Wiley & Sons, 1995
ISBN   047 1020567

The ABCs of Stock Speculation
S. A. Nelson, 1903. Reprinted by Fraser Publishing Company, 1984
ISBN   0 87034 054 9

The Stock Market Barometer
William P. Hamilton, Harper & Brothers 1922. Reprinted by Fraser Publishing Company, 1993
ISBN   0 87034 111 1

The Dow Theory
Robert Rhea, Barron's, 1932. Reprinted by Fraser Publishing Company, 1993
ISBN   0 87034 110 3

Technical Analysis of Stock Trends
Robert D. Edwards and John F. Magee, John Magee Inc., 1948 and subsequent editions. Seventh Edition 1997
ISBN   0 814403 735

Technical Analysis of Stocks and Commodities

Taking Stock of Commodity Trading Methods by B. Venitis
Vol. 1:6 (129-132), 1982/3

A 'map' for the trading jungle by G.D. Noble
Vol. 4:2 (81-82), 1986

Real world technical analysis by K. Calhoun
Vol. 9:3 (103-103), 1991

Dow Theory by M.F. Bowman and T. Hartle
Vol. 8:9 (359-363), 1990

Financial Times
A series of articles by Gillian O'Connor in Weekend Money

Picking the pops from the charts	19.8.95
How the trend can become your friend	2.9.95
How candlesticks can shed light on trends	9.9.95
Indicators confirm your first thoughts	16.9.95
Waves that boom and crash	30.9.95
Simple approaches to a complex jigsaw	14.10.95
In search of the stars	21.10.95

Investors Chronicle
A series of articles by Robin Griffiths

Making a science of an art form	8.9.95
The pencil is mightier than the PC	15.9.95
What are the charts telling us now	22.9.95

RFT Web Site at http://www.wiley-rft.reuters.com
This is the series' companion web site where additional quiz questions, updated screens and other information may be found.

Quick Quiz Answers

1. Indicate "true" or "false" as to whether the following statements are underlying principles of technical analysis.

	True	False
a) The main focus is on what ought to happen in the market		✔
b) Patterns exist in market behaviour	✔	
c) History repeats itself	✔	
d) Market action discounts nothing		✔

2. According to Dow Theory, briefly describe what is happening in the various phases of a major trend numbered 1 to 6 in this diagram.

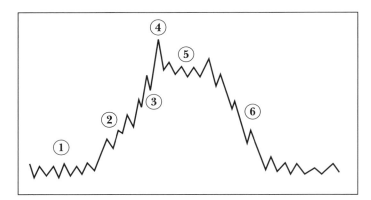

① Phase 1: **Accumulation** where price action is moving sideways

② Phase 2: **Uptrend** where investors begin to participate

③ Phase 2: **Corrections** or **pullbacks** to market prices

④ Market **peak**

⑤ Phase 3: **Accumulation** period after peak

⑥ Phase 3: End marked by a **downtrend**

Your notes

This section of the book should take about 90 minutes to hours of of study time. You may not take as long as this or you may take a little longer – remember your learning is individual to you.

The Will Rogers theory has only two rules.
Rule 1: If it don't go up, don't buy it.
Rule 2: If it don't go down, don't sell it.

The Will Rogers Theory of Point and Figure Trading by J. Adam Hewison
Technical Analysis of Stocks and Commodities, Vol. 9:8 (320-322), 1991

Introduction

The technical analyst has a wide variety of technical analysis tools and techniques to choose from. All of them require some type of chart plotting. Charts can be plotted by hand as you have already carried out, or more likely today, charts are produced with computer applications such as Reuters Graphics and Reuters 3000 products.

Although this wide choice exists, most technical analysts tend to have favoured chart types and analytical methods that they prefer to use.

Over time, experienced analysts develop a "feel" for the way one type of chart represents market action and may tend to use it predominantly. Each different chart type offers a different perspective to market action though and analysts tend to work comfortably with several chart types to ensure the greatest depth to their analysis. Thus, all analysts learn to use a variety of available chart types.

This section of the book covers the basic types of charts that are available, how analysts create them and how analysts use them. Charts may be relatively simple to create, or much more complex. Chart types range from simple line or bar charts, to point and figure charts, to the more involved candlestick charts which actually originated in Japan centuries ago. Each type of chart is valuable because it highlights or emphasizes a different aspect of pricing. For example, while line charts are the simplest form of chart, connecting consecutive closing prices, they show the results of market movements over a given time period. The candlestick chart shows Open/High/Low/Close prices and provides edited highlights of what happened in a particular market.

The chart types covered include:

- Line (closing price only, open interest and most indicators)
- Bar (open/high/low/close price)
- Candlestick (open/high/low/close price)
- Point and Figure (price changes)
- Histogram (volume and some indicators)

For some of these chart types there are activities for you to carry out to illustrate particular points – you will benefit if you take the time to perform the activities, but if you do not have time then the answers are always illustrated. You may find it useful to use a pencil for these activities – it's a lot easier to erase any mistakes! You may also find it useful to photocopy the original blank charts as a backup.

Each chart type is discussed using the following process:

 What is it?

 How is it used?

 Important information

 Useful diagrams

 Examples

The **line chart** is the simplest form of chart joining a series of points for instrument data on the vertical axis (Y-axis) and a timescale on the horizontal axis (X-axis).

Line charts are not frequently used today. Typically Bid, Ask, High, Low or Close prices are used for the vertical axis and timescales used can vary from tick (every price plotted consecutively) to hourly, daily and weekly.

There are a number of ways in which line chart data can be plotted – two involve the vertical axis and one the timescale.

Arithmetic Vertical Scale

The most common method is to use an arithmetic scale where each division represents the same price difference. This is appropriate wherever the range on the price scale is not great. In derivative markets and for short-term trading on equity markets, arithmetic scale is suitable most of the time.

Logarithmic Vertical Scale

This method uses a price scale where the Y-axis is constructed using a logarithmic scale. The chart still uses an arithmetic timescale so the chart is often termed **semi-logarithmic**. The main purpose for using a logarithmic scale is to keep price movements involving very large rises and falls in perspective. In the equity market, many players believe that it is better to chart stocks which have seen very large rises/falls in prices using a logarithmic Y-axis rather than using an arithmetic scale.

Timescale

Timescales can vary from recording every trade, to showing only the last trade for each month. Shown opposite are the two most common price scales, the last price for each day on the left and the last price for each week on the right. Notice how the daily chart shows more detail, but the weekly chart is less cluttered, revealing the larger picture. Technical analysts choose the timescale that is most appropriate for the time horizon of their analysis or trading.

Arithmetic Chart   Semi-Log Chart

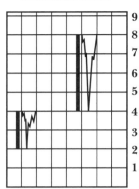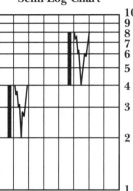

In both cases a movement from 2 – 4 and 4 – 8 is 100%. In the arithmetic chart the movement looks twice as big as it really is. In the semi-logarithmic chart the movements look the same. Why not measure the line lengths to check?

Arithmetic Charts

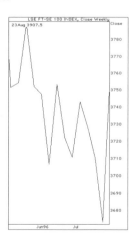

These charts illustrate prices over the same period of time, but the left shows the data in terms of daily closing prices, and the right shows the data in terms of weekly closing prices.

Arithmetic Chart

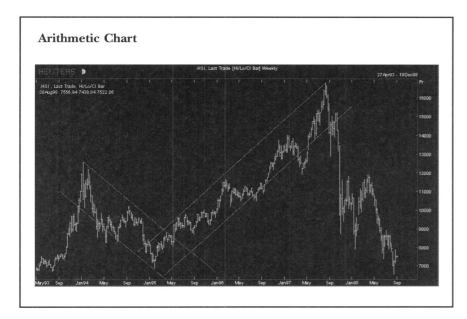

These charts show the weekly bar charts for the Hang Seng Index. The top chart shows the share prices plotted on an arithmetic scale; the bottom chart shows the same prices using a semi-logarithmic scale. The channels which are indicated by the diagonal lines give an indication of the difference in appearance of the price movements. The semi-log chart illustrates more clearly the absolute change in prices.

Semi-logarithmic Chart

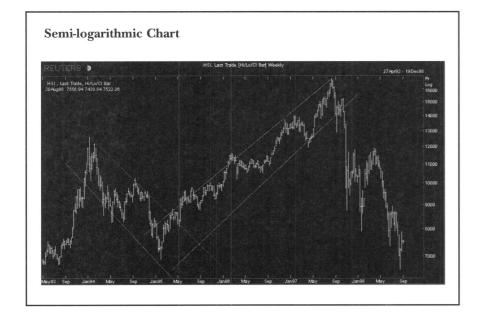

Exercise 2a
Using the blank Arithmetic and Semi-logarithmic charts and closing prices for Iomega Corporation, plot the data and compare the charts.

Exercise 2b
Using the blank charts, daily and weekly closing prices for the FT-SE 100 Index, plot the data and compare the charts.

Iomega Corp daily closing prices

Day	Price
1	10.00
2	10.63
3	10.50
4	10.44
5	10.25
6	10.25
7	10.50
8	10.00
9	10.38
10	10.00
11	10.38
12	11.00
13	13.25
14	13.75
15	14.50
16	15.00
17	15.00
18	14.13
19	14.75
20	14.50
21	14.50
22	14.13
23	13.88
24	14.50
25	15.25
26	14.75
27	14.63
28	14.25
29	14.13
30	14.63
31	15.31
32	16.50
33	18.00
34	22.00
35	23.25
36	20.00
37	21.00
38	21.50
39	20.25
40	21.00

Arithmetic Chart

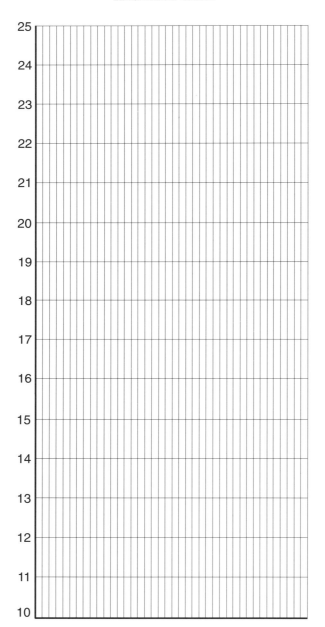

Semi-Logarithmic Chart

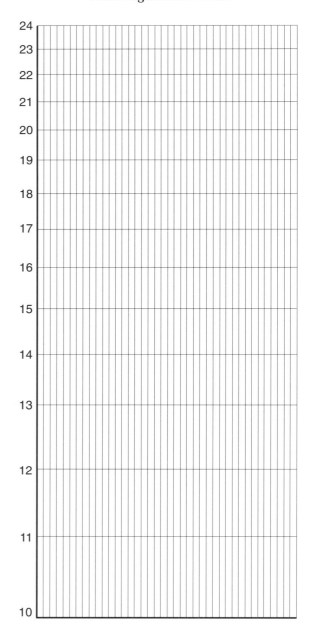

FT-SE100 Index daily closing prices

Day	Price
1	3776
2	3752
3	3723
4	3707
5	3728
6	3754
7	3759
8	3776
9	3754
10	3790
11	3778
12	3789
13	3764
14	3747
15	3752
16	3760
17	3775
18	3747
19	3748
20	3739

FT-SE 100 Index weekly closing prices

Week (= day above)	Price
2	3752
6	3754
10	3790
15	3752
19	3748

Daily Chart

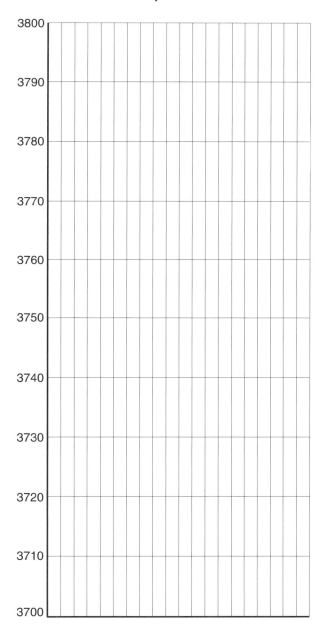

Weekly Chart

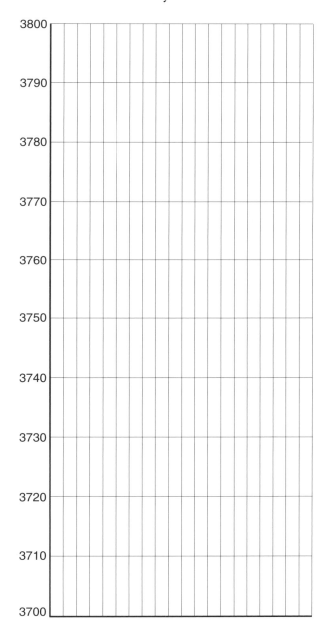

Exercise 2a
Your charts should have looked something like these.

Arithmetic Chart

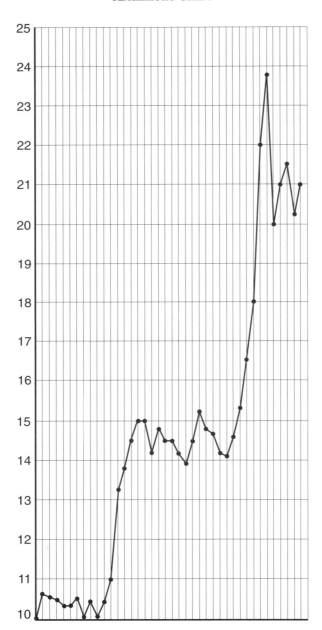

Semi-Logarithmic Chart

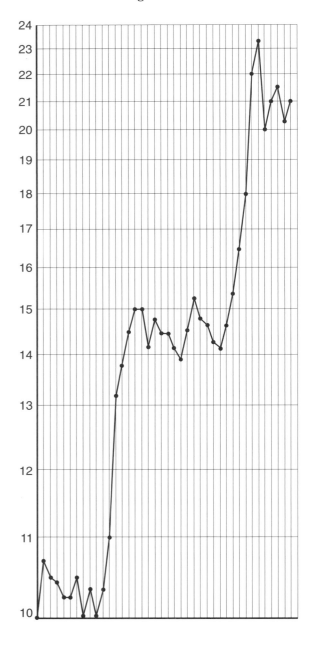

Exercise 2b
Your charts
should have
looked
something
like these.

Daily Chart

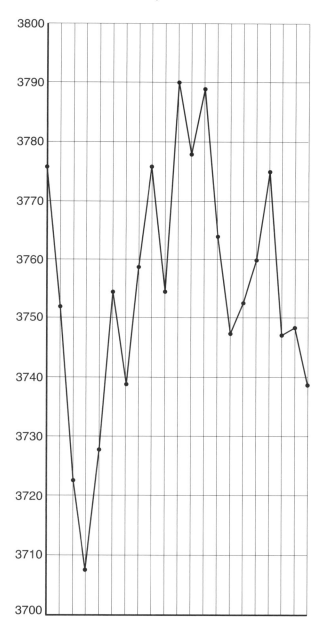

Weekly Chart

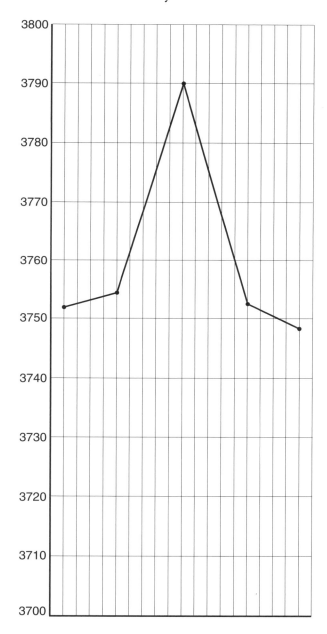

Bar Charts

The **bar chart** is the most common method used by western technical analysts to represent price action. A bar chart plots instrument data activity for each period as a series of vertical bars. The period may be anything from one minute to one year, depending upon the time horizon of the analysis.

In most cases, the period bar indicates **High, Low** and **Close** prices for historical data and **High, Low** and **Last** for real-time prices. Some bars indicate **Open/High/Low/Close** prices – especially for exchange traded instruments – but Open prices are not always available for historical data. Just as for line charts, bar charts can use an arithmetic or a logarithmic scale for the vertical axis. The analyst's choice of scale will be based on the same considerations as discussed in the previous section for line charts (eg, is trying to keep price movements in perspective). Nonetheless, arithmetic scales are still the most frequently used.

Drawing a Bar
Bars are drawn as follows:
1. Draw a **vertical** line between the **High** and **Low** prices.

2. Add a short bar to the **right** of the vertical bar as the **Close** or **Last** price (this bar is conventionally *twice the thickness* of the high-low vertical bar). The close price is, as its name implies, the price at the close of the market. When the market next opens and the financial instrument is traded once again the close price becomes the last price.

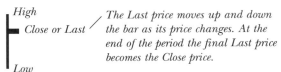

The Last price moves up and down the bar as its price changes. At the end of the period the final Last price becomes the Close price.

3. Add a short bar to the **left** of the vertical bar representing the **Open** price (this bar is conventionally *the same thickness* as the high-low vertical bar).

When used in charting futures the Open bar is often drawn shorter in length than that used for the Close.

Bar charts are useful because they convey more information than does a simple line chart, yet bar charts summarise the action for each period very economically. However, as illustrated in the charts on the next page, it is not always easy to read the bars when a lot of periods are displayed at once. Most charting software enables the analyst to zoom in and out to see more or less detail. Also, longer periods can be used to condense the number of bars displayed, without losing the overall picture. Analysts commonly use daily or shorter bars for trading purposes, and weekly or monthly charts for viewing the bigger picture.

During a strong **uptrend** the closing price will usually be near the price **High**.

If you see this pattern during a strong uptrend it is usually taken as a warning signal.

During a strong **downtrend** the closing price will usually be near the price **Low**.

If you see this pattern during a strong downtrend it is usually taken as a warning signal.

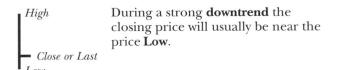

Prices on Reuters Graphics are displayed in the following order:

750	760	740	745
Open	High	Low	Close
			Market closed at 745

LME 3MONTH COPPER Daily

28Aug 1943.0 1943.0 1934.0 1941.0

A daily bar chart for LME Copper 3 month forward contract prices

This shows a magnified view of the area in the chart – you can see the bars more clearly

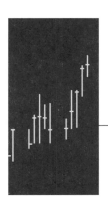

This shows a magnified view of the area in the chart – you can see the bars more clearly

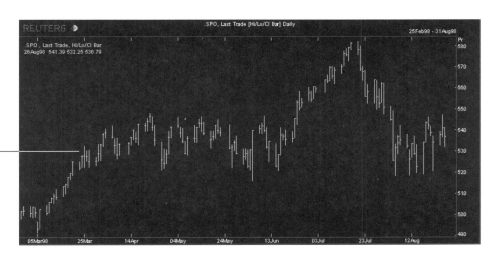

REUTERS

.SPO, Last Trade [Hi/Lo/Cl Bar] Daily

25Feb98 - 31Aug98

.SPO., Last Trade, Hi/Lo/Cl Bar
26Aug98 541.39 532.25 536.79

Candlestick Charts

 A **candlestick chart** shows the same data as is used for each period of a bar chart in a particular way that highlights the relationship between the opening and closing prices. Each period is represented by a **candle**, composed of its **real body** and its "**shadows**," (which are alternatively referred to as "wicks"). The **real body** is drawn using the **Open/Close** or Last prices and the **shadows** indicate the **High** and **Low** prices where they are outside the **Open/Close** range.

In addition, a candlestick provides a visual indication of the relative price movement of the instrument for the period.

❏ If the Close or Last is **lower** than the Open price then the candle body is coloured **black**

❏ If the Close or Last is **higher** than the Open price then the candle body is coloured **white** or **red** as used originally

 Although candlestick charts are a relatively recent introduction into western technical analysis, Japanese rice traders used these charts centuries ago. Many exponents of candlestick charts believe that patterns produced even by 2 – 3 days trading can give important signals for short-term trading markets such as futures.

 Drawing a Candlestick
Candlesticks are drawn as follows:
1. Draw a **vertical** line between the **High** and **Low** prices which is known as the **wick** or **shadow**.

2. Overlay on this wick a **candle** or **body** for which its top and bottom limits are given by its **Open** and **Close/Last** prices. If the Close is **lower** than the Open price, then colour the candle **black**. If the Close is **higher** than the Open, then leave the candle **hollow** or **white**.

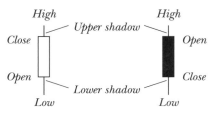

 Candlestick charts use what may seem a bewildering number of names for candles and their patterns. Below are just a few explanations of candles and patterns:

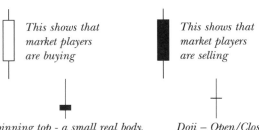

This shows that market players are buying

This shows that market players are selling

Spinning top - a small real body, with shadows longer (no more than 2-3 times) the real body

Doji – Open/Close are the same

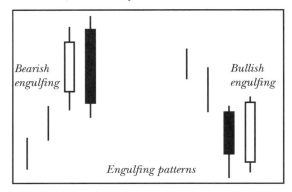

Bearish engulfing

Bullish engulfing

Engulfing patterns

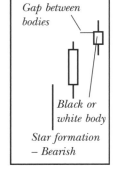

Gap between bodies

Black or white body

Star formation – Bearish

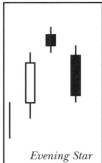

Evening Star

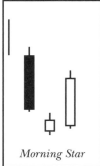

Morning Star

Candlestick Charts

WEEKLY NIKKEI 225 CANDLESTICK CHART

24Nov93 – 31Dec96

.N225 , Last Trade, Candle,
01Dec96 21276.30 21460.57 21020.36 21020.36

Pr
JPY

Evening Star

*Bearish engulfing – this
is also virtually an
Evening Star formation*

Morning Star

*A weekly candlestick chart of last trade
values for the Nikkei 225 index*

*Bullish
engulfing*

Point and Figure Charts

Point and figure charting is a simple technique for plotting the price action in any market in order to identify patterns and trends. The charts are simple and easy to construct, involve no timescale and only involve price changes of a user determined amount.

Prior to the introduction of computerised techniques this was probably one of the most popular techniques due to its simplicity – it is still a tool used in futures pits. The convention is to plot a chart in vertical columns where the vertical axis consists of **boxes** and the scale is known as the **box size**. For example, a user may decide that each box represents one point in some circumstances and three points in another. **Xs** and **Os** are used to chart price movements. As prices rise an X is placed on the chart for each price rise equal to the chosen box size. An O is used for each price decline equal to the chosen box size. A second parameter used is the number of boxes that constitute a **reversal**. A key feature of these charts over other charts is that the horizontal axis (X-axis) is **not** time dependent. For this reason changes in day are often marked by the day number or by a colour change.

Choosing the Box Size

A small box size and small box reversal number will tend to give a large number of X and O columns. The chart can be made coarser by either raising the box size itself or the number of boxes that constitute a reversal. It is more common to increase the box size than the box reversal number – and while a one-box reversal may be used, a **multi-box** or **three-box reversal** is most common.

Depending upon the box size and reversal number, a point and figure chart could cover a day's trading or trading over several months.

Starting the Chart

The chart is started by placing a dot in the first box corresponding to the instrument price. Everytime the price rises (or falls) by the selected box size an X (or O) is placed in the **same** column. Xs (or Os) are marked in boxes to the value of the move.

 Xs and Os

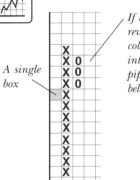

A single box

If the box size is 5 pips and a three box reversal is chosen, then the rising market X column would have a new column of three Os introduced alongside it if the price fell by 15 pips. The first O would be placed immediately below the highest X of the previous column.

Xs marked to the value of the price rise

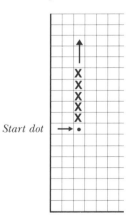

Start dot

Start dot

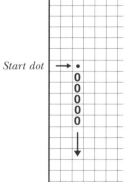

Os marked to the value of the price fall

Point and Figure Charts

Charting

Xs (or Os) are placed in the boxes until there is a price reversal and the price falls (or rises) by the selected box size. The chart now moves to the **next** column when there are two or more X or O symbols in it.

If the price **rises**, thus moving from O to X, then the X is placed above the O, or if there is already an X or O there, it is placed **one box across and up** from the last O.

The horizontal axis is therefore a series of columns showing up and down price movements. Price movements of less than the point size selected are filtered out.

Uses

Point and figure charts are used to indicate buy/sell signals and to identify the following:

Market behaviour	Point and figure chart
Demand exceeding supply	Long up columns – Xs
Supply exceeding demand	Long down columns – Os
Supply and demand in balance	Short up and down columns moving sideways

Price fall –
- *Move one column to right*
- *Move down a box for first O*
- *Mark as many Os as necessary the price fall*

Price rise –
- *Move one column to right*
- *Move up a box for first X*
- *Mark as many Xs as necessary for the price rise*

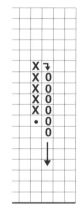

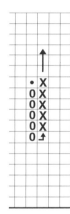

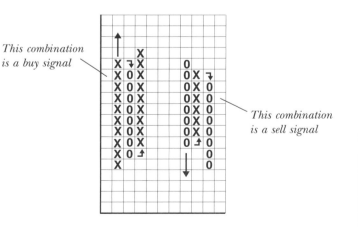

This combination is a buy signal

This combination is a sell signal

Point and Figure Charts

An Example

The following is a list of prices which are to be plotted on a point and figure chart. A chart using a box size of one and a three box reversal is required.

Prices

15   25   10   15   10   15   5   15   12   15

In all cases the price changes are greater than 3 so Xs and Os are required for every price movement. A chart with a box range 5 to 25 will be sufficient for the plot.

The chart is started by placing a dot in box 15 and then placing Xs in the first column up to 25.

At this point the price reverses by more than 3 points – it goes down to 10. Therefore an O is placed in the next column, one box down and Os continued down to 10.

The price reverses again to 15. Now an X is placed in the next column, one box up and Xs continued to 15.

You have probably got the idea by now. Why not check the rest of the chart?

It is worth remembering that if the price does not rise or fall by the selected box size, then no entry is required. A point and figure chart only records price movement – it is not dependent on time.

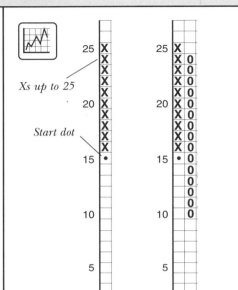

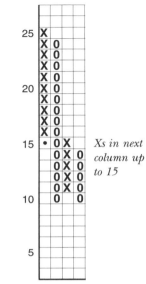

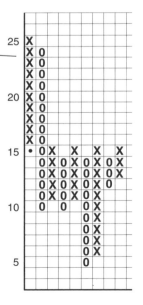

Point and Figure Charts

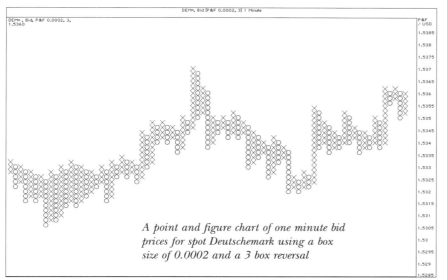

A point and figure chart of one minute bid prices for spot Deutschemark using a box size of 0.0002 and a 3 box reversal

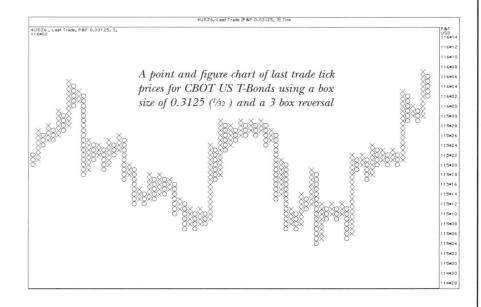

A point and figure chart of last trade tick prices for CBOT US T-Bonds using a box size of 0.3125 (¹/₃₂) and a 3 box reversal

Exercise 3
Plot the Reuters data as a point and figure chart.

Use a box size of 2 and a three box reversal.

You can check your answer on page 50.

Day	Price	Day	Price
1	766.5	26	797
2	770	27	784
3	769	28	789
4	758	29	789
5	751	30	779
6	749	31	778
7	753.5	32	770
8	777	33	765
9	794	34	765
10	782	35	756
11	764	36	750.5
12	771	37	747
13	773	38	755
14	773	39	751.5
15	761	40	756
16	752	41	746
17	758	42	746
18	750	43	756
19	743	44	762
20	745	45	777
21	747	46	781
22	764	47	777
23	789	48	767
24	780	49	767
25	792	50	760.5

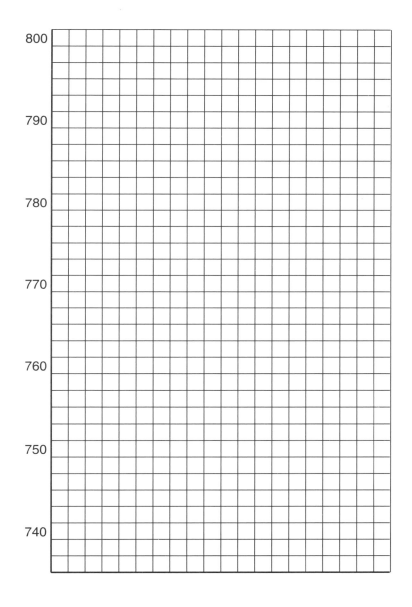

Volume Histogram Charts

Volume represents the total trading activity in a specific period for a commodity or financial instrument. For example, overall volume is the total number of contracts traded during the day of all contract months of the LIFFE FTSE-100 futures contract; also, it is the total number of Reuter ordinary shares that are bought and sold during the day on the London Stock Exchange. Usually the volume is displayed as a histogram (vertical bars rising from the zero scale grid line), below a line, bar or candlestick chart, such that the price and volume plots are lined up vertically for each period. The greater the volume the higher the vertical bar.

Volume charts give a measure of the amount of buying and selling that is taking place in a market. In the first section of the book, we saw that a basic tenet of Dow Theory is:

Volume must confirm the trend.

The Dow Theory places some emphasis on volume as a method of confirming market signals and trends. Volume is also a useful measure of the strength of price movements. High volume acts as a confirmation of price direction. Low volume tends to be a warning of lack of market interest at that price level and hence a risk that the price direction may change.

When using volume charts to confirm price directions it is useful to remember that market volumes can be **light** immediately before market holidays or before the release of major market statistics.

Drawing a Volume Chart

The most common way of drawing a volume chart is as a sub-plot on the same chart as that used to plot the data for a line, bar chart, etc. for prices. The volume data is usually plotted at the bottom of the price chart using the same horizontal time axis. The vertical axis (Y-axis) is usually an arithmetic scale that fits beneath the main chart.

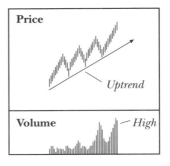

If prices are in uptrend and volumes high, then this is taken as confirming the direction of the trend

If prices are in uptrend but volumes are low, then this may indicate that buyers are losing interest and a trend change is on the way

Volume is seldom used by itself but in conjunction with chart patterns and indicators which are described later in the relevant sections. The following chart summarises the basic market signals that can be gauged from price/volume charts:

Price	Volume	Market
↑	↑	Strong
↑	↓	Warning sign
↓	↑	Weak
↓	↓	Warning sign

Warning sign indicates that the price trend may change.

Volume Histogram Charts

RTR.L, Last Trade [Bar], Volume(Last Trade) [Histogram] Daily   22Dec95 – 07Dec96

RTR.L , Last Trade, Bar,
29Nov96 724 729 718 725

If prices are in uptrend and volume rises when price rises and falls when price falls, volume is confirming the trend.

RTR.L , Volume(Last Trade), Histogram
29Nov96 1472635

USc1, Close, Marketvol Daily

15Nov 115●05

If prices are in uptrend but volume does not rise when price rises, volume is not confirming the trend.

This continuation futures chart shows the volume data for the front month contracts which are joined together

13Nov 481320

Open Interest Line Charts

Open interest is the total number of contracts which are still outstanding in a futures market for a specified futures contract. A futures contract is formed when a buyer and a seller take opposite positions in a transaction. This means that the buyer goes long and the seller goes short. Open interest is calculated by looking at **either** the total number of outstanding long or short positions – not both. Open interest is therefore a measure of contracts that have **not** been matched and closed out. The number of open long contracts must equal exactly the number of open short contracts. It is worth remembering that the reason a player holds an open futures position may be for hedging rather than speculative purposes. The following chart summarises how changes in open interest may result.

Action	Resulting open interest
New buyer (long) and new seller (short) trade to form a new contract	**Rise**
Existing buyer sells and existing seller buys – the old contract is closed	**Fall**
New buyer buys from existing buyer. The existing buyer closes his position by selling to new buyer	**No change** – there is no increase in long contracts being held
Existing seller buys from new seller. The existing seller closes his position by buying from new seller	**No change** – there is no increase in short contracts being held

Open interest acts as a confidence measure between bulls and bears in a market. A decline in open interest signals that either bulls or bears are closing their open positions which are not being matched by fresh positions being opened by new bulls or bears. An increase in open interest marks increased market participation by bulls or bears and is normally seen as a validation of any existing price trend.

Drawing an Open Interest Chart

Open interest data are usually plotted, together with volume data, at the bottom of a price chart. **Actual** open interest data is drawn as a **solid** line. However, open interest for certain commodity contracts, for example, Orange Juice, can have **seasonal tendencies** which should be taken into account. This is done by plotting the average open interest as a **dotted** line. It is the difference between actual and seasonal open interest lines that gives significance to any changes in open interest.

The solid line is moving above the dotted line which confirms the uptrend

Actual open interest – solid line

Average open interest – dotted line

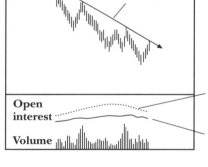

The solid line is moving below the dotted line which confirms the downtrend

Average open interest – dotted line

Actual open interest – solid line

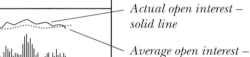

Price	Open Interest	Market
↑	↑	Strong
↑	↓	Warning sign
↓	↑	Weak
↓	↓	Warning sign

This chart summarises the basic market signals that can be gauged from price/open interest charts.

Warning sign *indicates that the Open interest is not supporting the price direction.*

Open Interest Line Charts

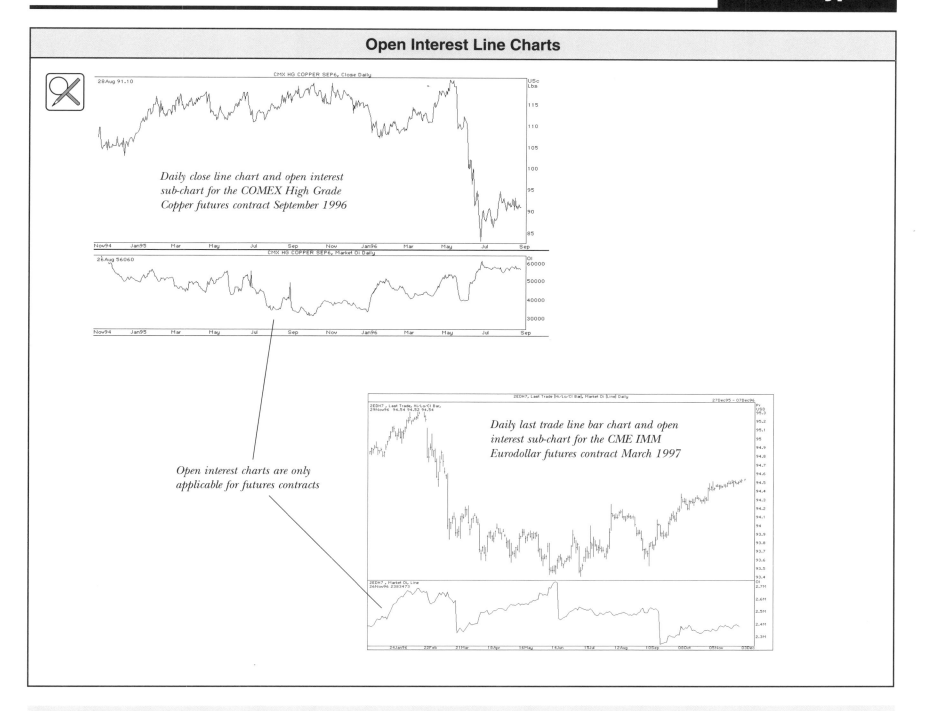

Daily close line chart and open interest sub-chart for the COMEX High Grade Copper futures contract September 1996

Open interest charts are only applicable for futures contracts

Daily last trade line bar chart and open interest sub-chart for the CME IMM Eurodollar futures contract March 1997

Exercise 3
Your charts
should have
looked
something
like these.

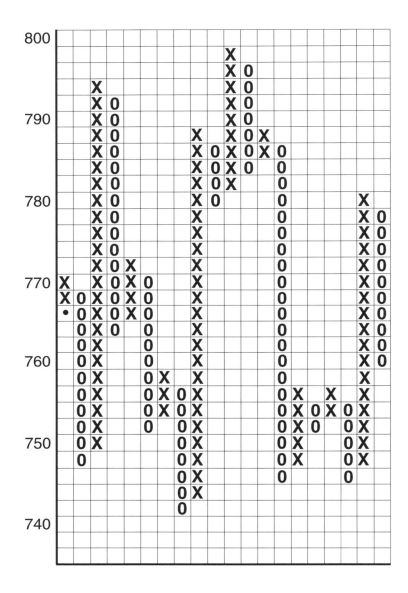

Charting Exercises

Chart Exercise 1

Shown opposite are three charts for Cadbury shares covering the same two year period. One is a daily chart, one is a weekly chart and the other is a monthly chart. Identify which chart is which.

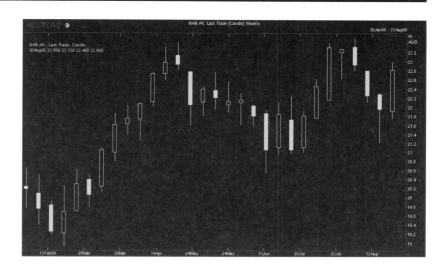

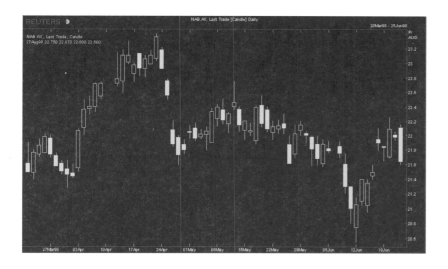

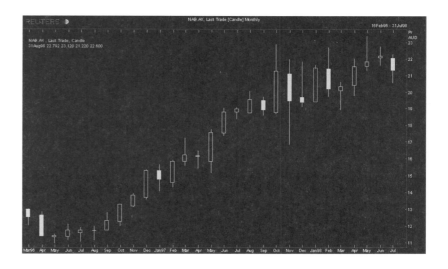

Chart Exercise 2
Identify which of these three charts shows price only, which one shows price and volume and which one shows price and open interest.

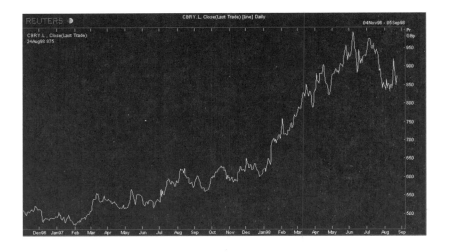

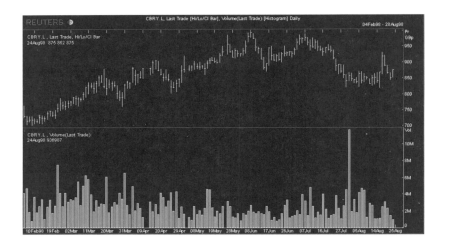

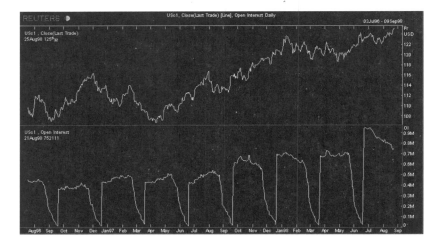

Summary

You have now finished the second section of the book and you should have a clear understanding of the following charts:

- Line

- Bar

- Candlestick

- Point and figure

- Histogram (eg, volume)

As a check on your understanding of this section, you should try the Quick Quiz Questions. You may also find the Overview section to be a helpful learning tool.

Quick Quiz Questions

1. For each of the following diagrams indicate the location of the High/Low/Open/Close prices.

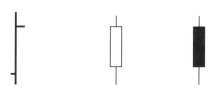

2. Match the following statements concerning Point and Figure charts.

A. Demand exceeding supply	**1.** Long down columns – Os
B. Supply exceeding demand	**2.** Short up and down columns moving sideways
C. Supply and demand in balance	**3.** Long up columns – Xs

A &		**B** &		**C** &	

3. Which of the following statements are true and which are false concerning volume and open interest charts?

	True	False
a) Price up and volume up indicate a weak market		
b) Price up and volume down are a warning sign		
c) Price up and open interest up indicate a strong market		
d) Price down and open interest up indicate a weak market		

You can check your answers on page 56.

Overview

Line Charts

- Typically joins a series of Bid, Ask, High, Low or Close prices, open interest or indicator
- Vertical axis – Y-axis – can be an **Arithmetic** or **Logarithmic** scale
- Horizontal axis – X-axis – can be tick, hour, day, week, month etc

Bar Charts

- Instrument prices plotted as a series of **vertical bars**
- Bar can indicate Open/High/Low/Close or Last prices

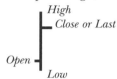

Point and Figure Charts

- Plot of stock or commodity prices which charts significant changes using a vertical axis of **boxes** and a scale known as the **box size**
- Price **rise** indicated by an **X** when the movement equals the box size
- Price **fall** indicated by an **O** when the movement equals the box size
- Typical charts use a **three box reversal**

Market behaviour	Point and Figure chart
Demand exceeding supply	Long up columns – Xs
Supply exceeding demand	Long down columns – Os
Supply and demand in balance	Short up and down columns moving sideways

Chart Types

Candlestick Charts

- Prices are plotted as **candles**. The **real body** indicates the **open/close** or **last** prices. The **shadows** indicate the high and low prices
- If the close or last price is **lower** than the open price, then the real body of the candle is **black**
- If the close or last price is **higher** than open price, then the real body of the candle is **white** or **red**

Open Interest Line Charts

- ❑ Line plot of **total number of contracts still outstanding** in a futures market for a specified contract month
- ❑ Open interest is calculated by either looking at the total number of outstanding long or short positions – **not both**

Price	Open Interest	Market
↑	↑	Strong
↑	↓	Warning sign
↓	↑	Weak
↓	↓	Warning sign

Volume Histogram Charts

- Vertical bars representing the **total trading activity** in a specific period for a commodity or financial instrument – the greater the volume the higher the vertical bar
- Measure of the amount of **buying** and **selling**

Price	Volume	Market
↑	↑	Strong
↑	↓	Warning sign
↓	↑	Weak
↓	↓	Warning sign

Further Resources

Books

Japanese Candlestick Charting Techniques
Steve Nison, New York Institute of Finance, 1991
ISBN   0 1393 1650 7

Candlestick Charting Explained
Gregory Morris, Probus Publishing Co., 1995
ISBN   1 55738 891 1

Study Help for Point & Figure Techniques
Alexander Wheelan, Fraser Publishing, 1990
ISBN   0 8703 4091 3

Technical Analysis of Stock Trends Chapter 2
Robert D. Edwards and John Magee, John Magee Inc.
ISBN   0 910944 00 8

Technical Analysis of the Futures Markets Chapter 3
John J. Murphy, New York Institute of Finance, 1986
ISBN   0 13 898008 X

Technical Analysis of Stocks and Commodities

Technical Analysis of Volume by H.K. Waxenberg
Vol. 4:2 (65-68), 1986

Point and Figure Charting by G. van Powell
Vol. 11:1 (30-33), 1993

Candlesticks and Intraday Market Analysis by G.S. Wagner & B.L Matheny
Vol. 11:4 (169-173), 1993

RFT Web Site at http://www.wiley-rft.reuters.com
This is the series' companion web site where additional quiz questions, updated screens and other information may be found.

Quick Quiz Answers

Your notes

1. *For each of the following diagrams indicate the location of the High/Low/Open/Close prices.*

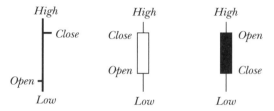

2. *Match the following statements concerning Point and Figure charts.*

   A. Demand exceeding supply

   1. Long down columns – Os

   B. Supply exceeding demand

   2. Short up and down columns moving sideways

   C. Supply and demand in balance

   3. Long up columns – Xs

A &	3	**B** &	1	**C** &	2

3. *Which of the following statements are true and which are false concerning volume and open interest charts?*

	True	False
a) *Price up and volume up indicate a weak market*		✓
b) *Price up and volume down are a warning sign*	✓	
c) *Price up and open interest up indicate a strong market*	✓	
d) *Price down and open interest up indicate a weak market*	✓	

This section of the book should take about 2 hours of study time. You may not take as long as this or you may take a little longer – remember your learning is individual to you.

The longer a trendline is in effect and the more data points that are used to establish the line, the greater the significance is. Significant penetration of the trendline usually indicates a reversal or a slowing of the trend.

On Trendlines, Money Flow Index and the Elliott Wave by Brian D. Green
Technical Analysis of Stocks and Commodities, Vol. 12:8 (321-324), 1994

Introduction

Charting the prices of a financial instrument creates a picture of the market "battle" between buyers (bulls) and sellers (bears). Market prices do not move in a straight line but zig-zag as prices rise and fall depending on who is winning the buyer/seller battle. In order to decide if they should buy or sell, market players need tools to determine their trading strategy. One such tool is the market **trend** and is simply defined as:

The direction of the market – the way the market is moving.

There are two basic **trend** directions plus the situation when a market is within a sideways **consolidation** to consider:

Uptrend

This is considered to be the time to **buy** or **go long**. A major uptrend is also known as a **Bull** market. Market players have the opportunity to profit by being **bullish** – buying and staying with the uptrend.

Downtrend

This is considered to be the time to **sell** or **go short**. A major downtrend is also known as a **Bear** market. Market players have the opportunity to profit by being **bearish** – selling with a view to buying later. In equity markets it is not always possible for normal investors to be short – they are either in or out of the market.

Sideways Market

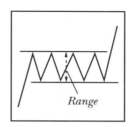

Range

This situation arises when there is no strong conviction by either bulls or bears. As a result market prices rise and fall in a more congested space – hence the term **congestion** or **consolidation** is sometimes used. This type of pattern is generally considered to be a signal to stay out of the market. However, some traders use congestion patterns as an opportunity for **range** trading – selling on the high side of the congestion and buying back and reversing long at the low side.

Sideways patterns eventually result in a **breakout** and reversal or continuation of the original trend. Reversals and continuations often form characteristic patterns which the technical analyst uses to make trading decisions. However, these patterns are not always easy to recognise!

Within the zig-zag trend patterns you may also see temporary corrections in price movements – these are known as **pullbacks**.

You have already been introduced to market sayings such as

The trend is your friend
Go with the trend

and as long as the trend is intact the situation is stable.

While the trend is intact, if you look carefully at the zig-zag pattern of the trend you may notice that it is possible to draw two more or less parallel lines – one joining the high points of the peaks and the other the lower points. These lines bound what is known as a trend **channel**.

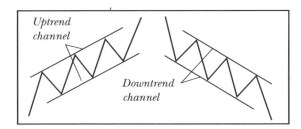

Both of the lines bounding a channel can be viewed as retaining 'walls' against which prices keep hitting and bouncing off. In an uptrending channel if the **lower** channel line is broken then this may warn of a possible reversal of the uptrend. If the **upper** channel line is broken then this suggests an acceleration and strengthening of the uptrend. In the case of a downtrend it is breach of the upper channel line that warns that the existing trend may be ending.

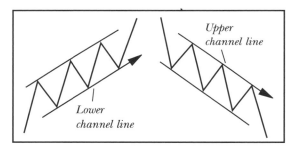

What is actually happening during these ups and downs in the zig-zag patterns? The patterns are caused by the constant battle between bulls and bears in the market place. At market peaks the bears gain ascendancy and take control, while in the troughs the situation is reversed and the bulls gain ascendancy. If market players move to stop a price fall, then they buy and provide **support** to the market. If they move to stop a price rise, then they sell and **resistance** to the rise is the outcome.

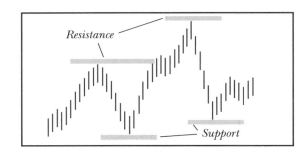

Observing how markets react to support and resistance is a good barometer of the measure of an underlying trend.

In any market there will be short, medium and long -term trends. In some cases all these trends work in the same direction resulting in a strongly trending market. In other cases the different trends conflict with each other which results in a much more subdued market price action. The essence of using trends for both long-term investors and short-term traders is to be able to assess when trends are likely to **change**.

Technical analysts are looking for a trendline to be broken — a **breakout**. This is a signal to examine charts and market events closely. The questions the analyst will be trying to answer include:

- Has the trendline/channel been broken?

- Are prices just fluctuating in their channel?

- Are there any pullbacks?

- Are prices moving sideways?

- Are there any continuation/reversal patterns?

So far the approach taken in considering patterns has only concerned trends. What would Dow have had to say about such an approach?

Although Dow Theory concentrates on trends in the market, any movement has to be **confirmed** – Dow used his stock indices and volume of trading for this purpose.

More modern techniques of pattern confirmation used by technical analysts include **moving averages**, which are another tool for analysing trends. An average is calculated for a number of prices by summing the prices and dividing the result by the number involved. For simple moving averages, the price is averaged over a number of days. On each successive day the oldest price drops out of the average and is replaced by the current price — hence the average moves daily. Exponential and weighted moving averages use the same technique but weight the figures — least weight to the oldest price, most to the current price.

Price	3 day moving average		
		20	
20	21.67	21	$(20 + 21 + 24) \div 3 = 21.67$
21	22.67	24	
24	24.00	23	
23	23.67		
25	22.67	20	
23		21	
20		24	$(21 + 24 + 23) \div 3 = 22.67$
		23	
		25	

Within moving average charts it is also possible to see price action moving within a channel with walls a certain percentage above and below the moving average. Conventional price channel analysis has the upper/lower bands as a fixed percentage above/below the underlying moving average. However, John Bollinger, the US technical analyst, has further developed this technique by introducing a volatilty measure such that the bands **broaden** in a volatile market and **constrict** in a market where trading is subdued. These bands are known as **Bollinger bands**.

Another type of chart which is used to confirm trends is based on **relative performance**. This is a measure of how well a particular instrument is performing relative to the rest of the market as gauged by comparing it with a broad market measure or another instrument. For example, if you have shares in Reuters Ltd you may want to see how well your shares are performing relative to the FT-Actuaries All-Share Index. A rising relative performance means that the share is outperforming the market whilst a falling value means the share is underperforming. In the equity market this performance measure is referred to as **relative strength** which should not be confused with the Relative Strength Index, which is an indicator described in the next section.

Careful inspection of daily charts may also indicate the presence of **gaps** or blank spaces in the price chart. For example, in an uptrending market, if the highest price for any one day is lower than the lowest price for the following day, then a gap will appear in the chart. True gaps are an indication of a bull/bear market conviction which is so strong that a given price range has been completely ignored. Gaps are often seen in futures markets and to a lesser extent in equity markets. Gaps are rarely seen in 24-hour markets such as the spot FX majors for USD/DEM etc.

In order to help you identify the basic patterns that have been discussed here, and to give an overview of how technical analysts use them, information is given on the following:

- Trendlines/channels
- Continuation/consolidation patterns
- Reversal patterns
- Support and resistance
- Moving averages
- Relative performance/strength
- Gaps

The format for each section follows the same as adopted for the previous section.

It is important to remember that this book is not an exhaustive treatment of chart patterns – it only provides an overview to the subject. If you want to find out more about chart analysis, refer to the **Further Resources** listing at the end of this section.

Trendlines

 A **trendline** is a line connecting consecutive high or low data points in order to identify the direction of a market. The more frequently a trendline touches or closely approaches price highs or lows and the longer it continues to remain unbroken, the more significant the trend.

 Trendlines are used to identify the following characteristics in market trends:

- Direction of the trend
- Reversal of a trend
- Continuation of a trend
- Support and resistance

A break of the trend line signals a weakening of the trend. This is not necessarily a signal to buy or sell immediately, but rather a signal to be aware that a change may be occurring.

Uptrend
This is a line drawn joining **low** data points. It is drawn **under** the low points and connects at least **three consecutive rising low points**. Classically the line does not cross any other data points but recent research shows this is permissible under certain conditions.

Downtrend
This is a line drawn joining **high** data points. It is drawn **above** the high points and connects at least **three consecutive falling high points**. Classically the line does not cross any other data points but recent research shows this is permissible under certain conditions.

Reversal
This is when the validity of the current trend ends and the trendline is broken. Immediately following a reversal it is quite common for the market to move sideways. However, there are instances where the end of a trend is followed by a violent and strongly trending market in an opposite direction to the original trend.

Continuation/Consolidation
Prices often fluctuate back and forth towards the trendline giving rise to a number of patterns such as pennants and triangles. The sideways trend produced is generally an indication of a temporary pause in the prevailing trend.

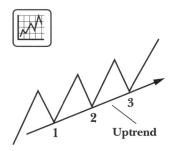

For an uptrend the line is drawn below the data points. Consecutive low points must be higher than the previous point, for example, 2 is higher than 1.

For a downtrend the line is drawn above the data points. Consecutive high points must be lower than the previous point, for example, 2 is lower than 1.

Traditionally, in uptrends and downtrends the line does not cross any other data points. However, new research is introducing concepts on trendlines and channels that permit this.

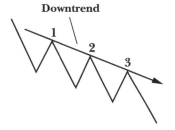

A common reversal showing a head and shoulders pattern

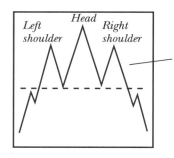

A flat top, or ascending, triangle continuation pattern

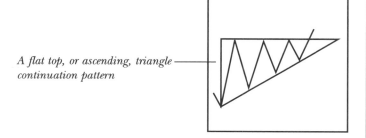

Trendlines

LSE REUTERS HLDGS, Close Daily

28Aug 772

Uptrend line – the more frequently the trendline touches or closely approaches the line and the longer it remains unbroken, the more significant the trend.

Downtrend line – the more frequently the trendline touches or closely approaches the line and the longer it remains unbroken, the more significant the trend.

ITL=, Bid Daily

28Aug 1513.00

A line chart of daily bid prices for the Italian lira against the US dollar

Continuation/Consolidation Patterns

Continuation patterns occur during periods of **consolidation** when prices are moving sideways following an up or down trend. The patterns are not always easy to recognise and do not always have the regular shapes described below! Continuation patterns have names based on geometric shapes:

- Triangles
- Rectangles
- Flags and pennants

Continuation patterns last for varying periods of time – flags and pennants only last a few days, rectangles can last up to a year.

Market players use continuation patterns to determine a **target price** for their trading strategy. This target price is the level they expect the market to reach following breakout of the consolidation and resumption of the continuation trend.

Triangles

These occur in both up and down trends and represent a battle between buyers and sellers. Triangles can have flat tops, flat bottoms or sloping sides, as with an equilateral triangle. For example, in this

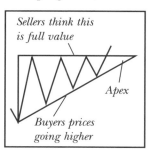

Sellers think this is full value

Apex

Buyers prices going higher

triangle the flat top indicates that the sellers think that the price is the full value, whereas the buyers are putting in orders for higher and higher prices. Eventually one side will win and a breakout will occur.

It is interesting that the closer the price gets to the apex of the triangle the less reliable the pattern becomes.

It is common to see that the breakout of a triangle following an uptrend gives rise to a short, sharp rise before a price fall occurs. Such breakouts are referred to as **bull traps** and quite often mark major bull market tops. In a downtrending market the inverse situation is called a **bear trap**, which often marks a major bear market bottom.

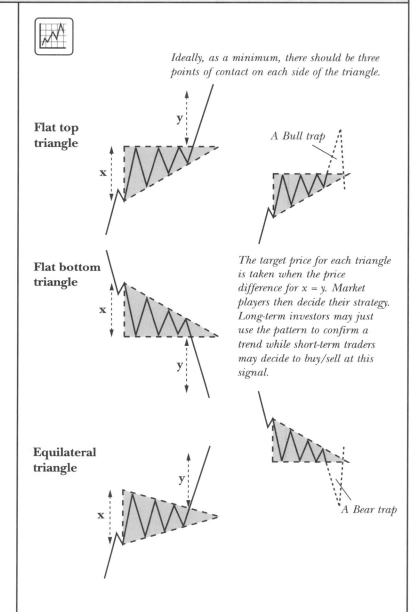

Ideally, as a minimum, there should be three points of contact on each side of the triangle.

Flat top triangle

y

x

A Bull trap

Flat bottom triangle

x

y

The target price for each triangle is taken when the price difference for x = y. Market players then decide their strategy. Long-term investors may just use the pattern to confirm a trend while short-term traders may decide to buy/sell at this signal.

Equilateral triangle

y

x

A Bear trap

Continuation/Consolidation Patterns

Rectangles

These represent a straight forward battle of support and resistance between buyers and sellers. Rectangles may build up over a period of months and last up to a year. If the breakout follows the direction of the trend then prices will continue to rise, but if the breakout is in the opposite direction then this should be considered a major reversal pattern. Sometimes after a breakout there is a small correction before a new trend direction is established. This correction, or **pullback**, retests the old resistance level which has now become support before the original trend direction is resumed.

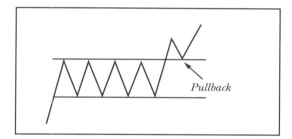

Pullback

Flags and Pennants

These are short-term patterns usually lasting no more than a few days and occur in fast-moving markets involving steep rises. They usually mark the half way point in a continuing price movement. Flags are shaped like downward sloping parallelograms while pennants are downward sloping and have a triangle like shape. The shapes are often difficult to identify but usually involve the following conditions:

- They occur after a sharp up or down price move
- The volume should decline for the duration of the pattern
- Prices should break out of the pattern within a few weeks otherwise it is unlikely that it is a flag or pennant

Rectangle

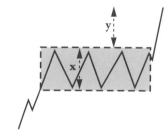

The target price for a rectangle is taken when the price difference for x = y as in the case for a triangle.

The target price for a flag or pennant is taken when the price difference for the flagpole, x, is reached in the direction of the trend following the breakout and trend continuation.

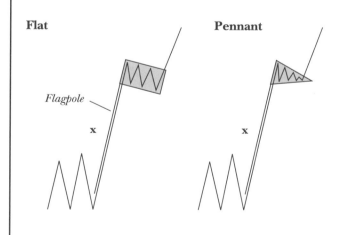

Flat

Pennant

Flagpole

x

x

Continuation/Consolidation Patterns

Bar chart of daily last trade prices for CBOT US T-Bond futures, December 1996

Bar chart of daily prices for Nikkei 225 Index

Bar chart of daily prices for GBP against USD

Line chart of daily close Shenzen 3 month Copper futures prices

Continuation/Consolidation Patterns

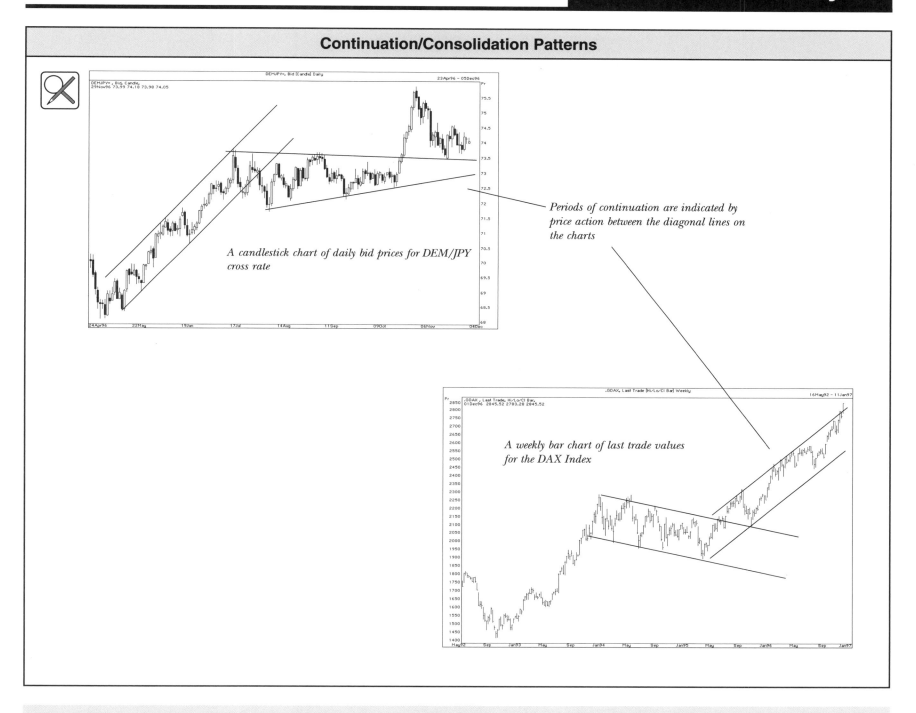

Periods of continuation are indicated by price action between the diagonal lines on the charts

A candlestick chart of daily bid prices for DEM/JPY cross rate

A weekly bar chart of last trade values for the DAX Index

Reversal Patterns

A **reversal pattern**, as the name implies, indicates a top or bottom in market prices accompanied by a trend reversal. Some of the patterns are relatively easy to identify and reliable in their interpretation – others are more complex. Reversal patterns are only important if they occur after a strong and marked up or down trend. A pattern observed after a downtrend is the **inverse**, or mirror image, of that seen after an uptrend although it is not always as prominent. The most common patterns which indicate market reversal are:

- Head and shoulders
- Double and triple tops/bottoms
- Wedges
- Rounding or saucer top/bottom – also known as 'scalloped'

Market players use reversal patterns to identify top and bottom price structures and select target prices for subsequent breakouts and reversals in market trends. To help establish a target price a technical analyst will draw a **neckline** which, in a head and shoulders pattern, is a line joining certain specified low points of the pattern.

Head and Shoulders

This pattern is made up of three peaks. The centre peak is higher than the outer two which are approximately the same height – the shape is supposed to resemble someone shrugging. The pattern usually occurs at the end of a long uptrend and is one of the most common and reliable of patterns. The left shoulder and head represent the struggle between buyers and sellers when high volumes are traded. At the appearance of the right shoulder, the volume should decline. The signal for completion of the pattern is price breaking below the neckline, which is a strong indication that prices will now trend downwards. Interestingly, an inverse head and shoulders in an equity market is often less pronounced and flatter than seen in an uptrend.

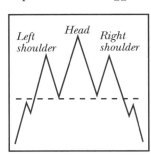

The neckline can be horizontal or slant up or down. More significance is attached to an upward sloping neckline in an uptrend than a downsloping one.

Head and shoulders

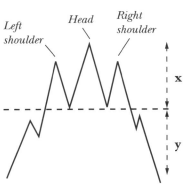

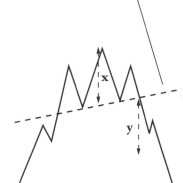

Inverse head and shoulders

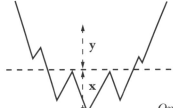

Once prices break through the neckline the target price for market players to take profit on positions taken at the breakout can be determined using the price difference x = y. This technique assumes that the price moved at least y prior to the emergence of the pattern.

Reversal Patterns

Double and Triple Tops/Bottoms

Double and triple tops and bottoms are successive peaks and troughs of approximately the same height and depth, which represent the continuing struggle of buyers and sellers to dominate the market. The patterns usually signal intermediate- or long-term changes in the trend. Eventually buyers or sellers win and the trend is reversed.

A double top looks like the letter M – a double bottom a W. Triple tops and bottoms resemble a head and shoulders but do not have such a pronounced head.

Double and triple tops/bottoms can be distinguished from head and shoulders patterns by looking at volumes, for example, the number of shares being traded. In double and triple tops/bottoms the volumes usually decrease for each peak, whereas in a head and shoulders pattern the volume at the formation of the right shoulder normally declines dramatically.

For a double top, a horizontal neckline is drawn through the support level at the low point of the mid-pattern trough.

Care is needed in using double and triple tops/bottoms as you need to be confident that the previous trend has been reversed. For example, two double top formations following each other could form part of a rectangular continuation pattern. It is worth noting that double and triple tops/bottoms need not have exactly equidistant peaks and troughs. Also, the peaks and troughs can be deep or shallow, though major tops and bottoms are usually associated with a deep consolidation area.

In general, double tops/bottoms occur more often than head and shoulders or triple tops/bottoms. However, the likelihood of a full reversal is greater with head and shoulders and triple tops/bottoms.

The neckline can be horizontal or slant up or down slightly.

Double top

Triple top

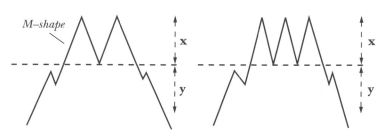

M–shape

Double bottom

Triple bottom

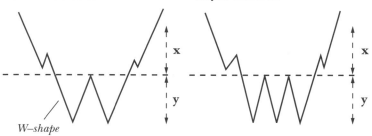

W–shape

Once prices break through the neckline the target level for the reversal can be determined taking the price difference x = y.

Reversal Patterns

Wedges

Triangles and wedges define converging prices before a reversal and can take several weeks or months to develop. These patterns are taken as signals of an opportunity to profit.

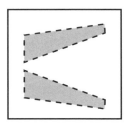

Wedges have boundaries that gently slope towards each other. Wedges can **rise** or **fall** – slope up or down. Just as with triangles, a wedge breakout should occur before the apex of the wedge is reached.

Rounding or Scalloped Bottom

These are not common types of reversal patterns. They tend to form slowly over a period of months indicating a protracted struggle between buyers and sellers with neither really gaining ascendancy.

A rounding top is roughly shaped like an umbrella canopy whereas a rounding bottom has a saucer shape. These patterns offer no clear-cut buy or sell signals but when considered in conjunction with fundamental analysis, technical analysts can use them to predict long-term investment opportunities.

Wedge

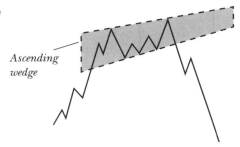

Ascending wedge

Rounding top

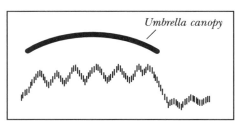

Umbrella canopy

Rounding or scalloped bottom

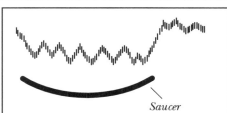

Saucer

Reversal Patterns

A bar chart of last trade weekly Nikkei 225 Index values

Double top

A bar chart of daily GBP/USD prices

Sloping neckline

Inverse head and shoulders

Left shoulder

Right shoulders

Head

Reversal patterns

Bar chart of daily prices for USD/DKK

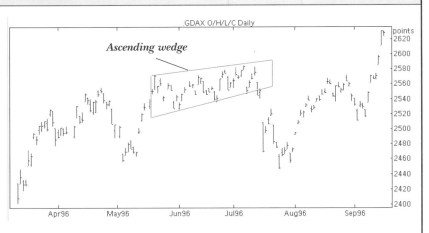

Bar chart of daily prices for DAX Index

Bar chart of daily last trade prices for CBOT US T-Bond futures for December 1996

Bar chart of daily last trade prices for Microsoft shares

Trendlines

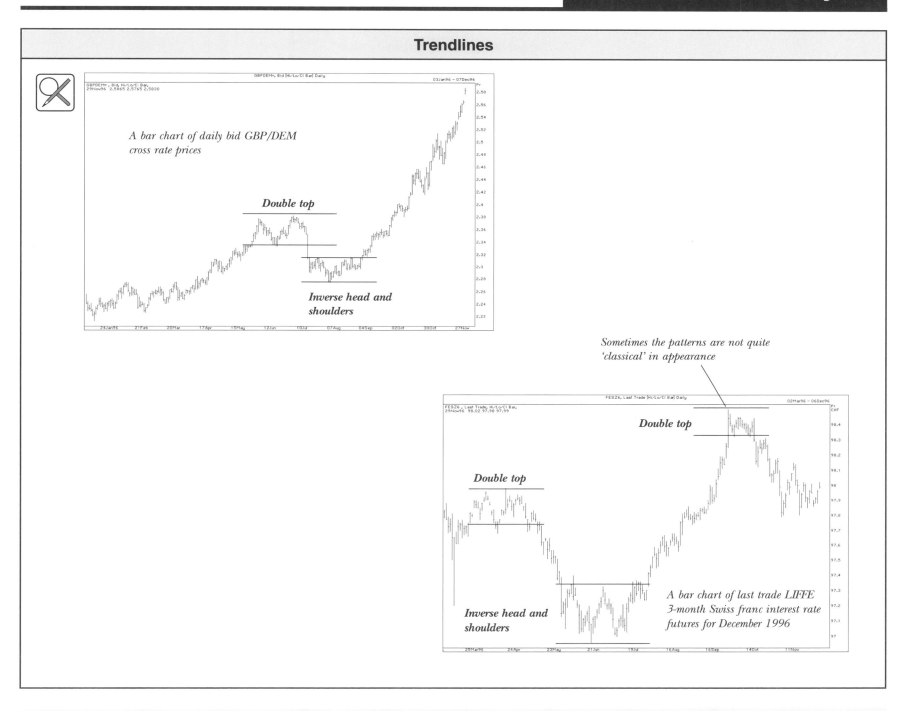

A bar chart of daily bid GBP/DEM cross rate prices

Double top

Inverse head and shoulders

Sometimes the patterns are not quite 'classical' in appearance

Double top

Double top

Inverse head and shoulders

A bar chart of last trade LIFFE 3-month Swiss franc interest rate futures for December 1996

Support and Resistance Lines

Support and **resistance lines** are one of the basic components of technical analysis and are important in the understanding of trends and their associated patterns such as continuations and reversals.

Support Level
This is the level that supports market price action for a period of time. It is the level where buying interest is strong enough to overcome selling pressure. The result is that the market does not fall below that level.

Resistance Level
This is the opposite of support and is the level that resists market price action for a period of time. It is the level where selling interest is strong enough to overcome buying pressure so the market does not exceed that level.

An idea essential to technical analysis is that the support and resistance levels are where the price movements stopped before. Traders expect that this is where prices will stop again, and if they do not, then the trends have failed.

Support and resistance lines are used by traders involved with both short- and long-term timescales. For example, futures traders tend to trade within the scope of the trading day, while equity traders have Daily/Weekly/Monthly timeframes. The performance of price action when support and resistance levels are approached is investigated closely by analysts for signals of continuation or a reversal of the previous trend.

If prices have been in an uptrend and then fall, breaking an important support level in the process, then this is taken as a warning of a trend reversal.

If a resistance level has been tested and not broken, then this is usually taken as an early warning of a possible trend change.

Support and resistance levels

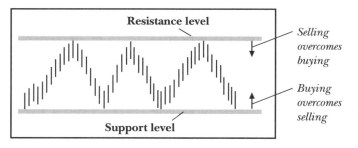

Resistance level

Selling overcomes buying

Buying overcomes selling

Support level

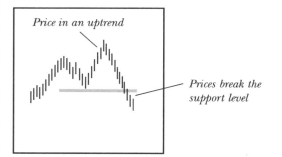

Price in an uptrend

Prices break the support level

Resistance level

If the resistance level is not broken the previous support may be challenged which may result in a trend change

Support and Resistance Lines

Support/Resistance Reversal

When a support level is broken then the level takes on the new role of resistance and when a resistance level is penetrated it takes on the new role of support.

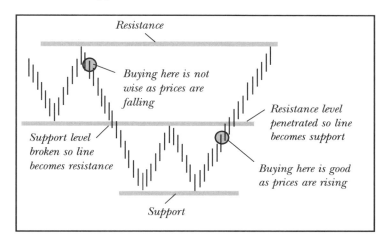

Resistance

Buying here is not wise as prices are falling

Support level broken so line becomes resistance

Resistance level penetrated so line becomes support

Buying here is good as prices are rising

Support

Open Interest – Future Markets

There is a relationship between support and resistance levels in an uptrend/downtrend. As a market moves away from support/resistance, that is, new buyers/sellers are entering the market then the open interest should **increase**. However, if such an increase is not observed, then this is taken as a warning signal.

Example of support/resistance reversal
A gold trader buys at $350 at A and sells his position at $400 – the resistance level, B. The market slides back to C, the support level at $360, and then rises quickly to D at $425. When should the trader buy? A popular price to buy back is at the $400 level – the previous resistance level, which may be expected to become the new support level. However, a sensible trader would have a stop loss level beneath the $400 level in case the expected support level failed to halt the downtrend in prices.

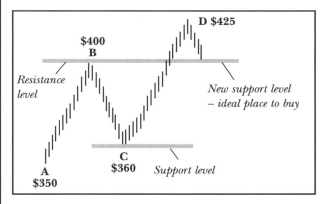

D $425

$400
B

Resistance level

New support level – ideal place to buy

C
$360 *Support level*

A
$350

Support and Resistance Lines

Retracement

As a market reacts or rallies following a strongly trending move, part of that price move is retraced – this is known as **retracement**. If the amount of retracement can be predicted then trading levels can be set to a trader's advantage. Technical analysts use **percentage retracements** to determine support and resistance levels. Quite often a correction in a trending market will retrace to approximately half or 50% of the previous move and so this figure is favoured by many traders. Other common retracements in a bull trend are approximately 33% and 66%.

As you will see in the later section on *Waves, Numbers and Cycles,* Gann charts and Elliott Wave Theory pay particular attention to retracements. Gann lines are often drawn in eighths or tenths and Elliott Wave Theory predicts retracement levels at 0.382 (about 33%) and 0.618 (about 66%), which are based on the reciprocals of the Fibonacci numbers 2.618 and 1.618 respectively.

Percentage retracements

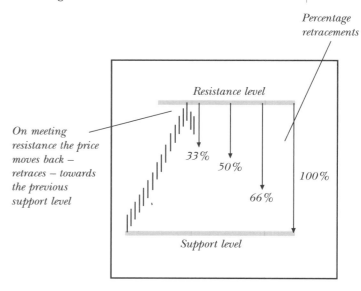

Percentage retracements

Resistance level

On meeting resistance the price moves back – retraces – towards the previous support level

33%

50%

66%

100%

Support level

Support and Resistance Lines

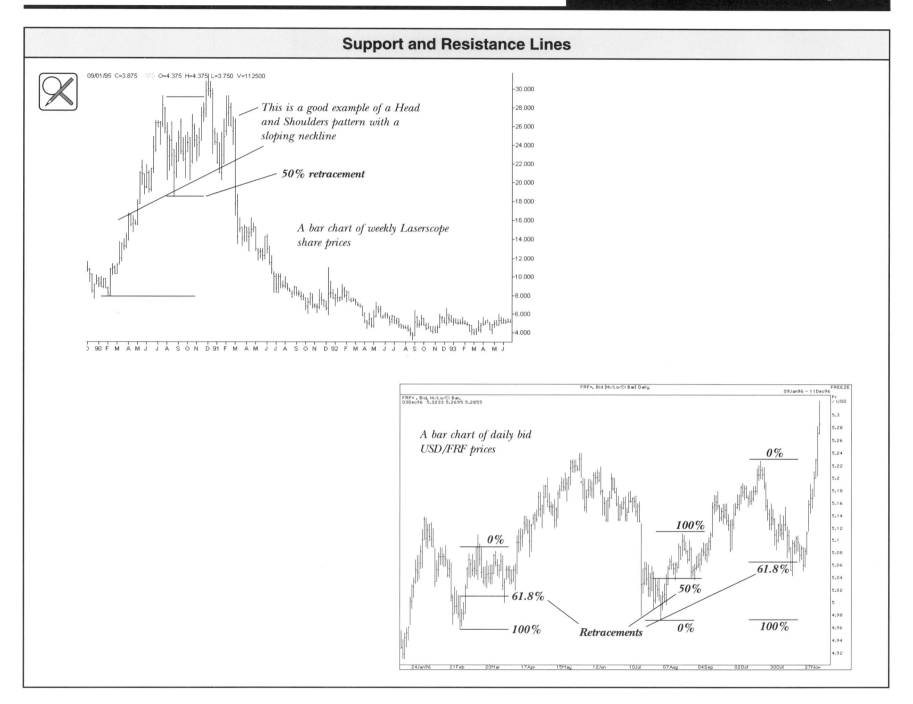

09/01/95 C=3.875 · 375 O=4.375 H=4.375 L=3.750 V=112500

This is a good example of a Head and Shoulders pattern with a sloping neckline

50% retracement

A bar chart of weekly Laserscope share prices

FRF=, Bid [Hi/Lo/Cl Bar] Daily

09Jan96 - 11Dec96 FREEZE

FRF=, Bid, Hi/Lo/Cl Bar,
03Dec96 5.3233 5.2695 5.2855

A bar chart of daily bid USD/FRF prices

0%

0%

100%

61.8%

61.8%

50%

100%

61.8%

Retracements

0%

100%

Moving Averages

A **moving average** is created by adding a series of closing prices and dividing by a particular number of periods. For simple moving averages, the price is averaged over a number of days. On each successive day the oldest price drops out of the average and is replaced by the current price - hence the average moves daily. Exponential and weighted moving averages use the same technique but weight the figures - least weight to the oldest price, most to the current price.

Price	3 day moving average
20	21.67
21	21.67
24	24.00
23	23.67
25	?
23	
20	

What is the next moving average in this sequence? You can check your answer on page 59.

A moving average is a lagging indicator that provides a way of 'smoothing out' data and which is used to confirm price trends. The period chosen for a moving average depends on the type of instrument being charted – the most common periods used are 9/10, 18/20, 40/50, 100 and 200 periods. Futures markets tend to use shorter-term moving averages, for example, 9 and 18 periods, whereas for long-term investments, such as equities, 50/100/200 are more popular periods. Assuming that the instrument being charted has a cyclical trading pattern, research has shown that the most successful moving average is associated with the cycle period for the instrument. There are three types of moving averages used widely, all having benefits and drawbacks, which are:

- Simple Moving Average (SMA)
- Weighted Moving Average (WMA)
- Exponential Moving Average (EMA)

In general, all three types of moving averages are used for the following:
- To detect trend directions
- To determine buy/sell signals

When using moving averages it is important to remember that you need to examine the relationship between the **actual price** and the **moving average**. This means that the plot for a moving average must appear on the price chart using the same X-axis as the instrument being analysed.

Trend directions

Bullish

Prices above moving average

Moving average line

The position of the moving average plot can be used to indicate the trend direction of a market

Bearish

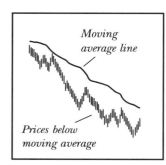

Moving average line

Prices below moving average

Market signal	Price/moving average relationship
Bullish	Prices **above** moving average and moving average moving **up**
Bearish	Prices **below** moving average and moving average moving **down**

Moving Averages

Using classical chart analysis techniques for a single moving average, the signal for buying is taken as the moving average turning **up** with price action **above** the moving average. However, trading using such a strategy can result in severe losses if the market prices oscillate violently – known as 'whipsawing'. In an attempt to avoid losses, analysts use a two moving average **crossover** technique to indicate buy/sell signals. The two moving averages typically comprise a short-term 5-10 period and a longer-term 15-35 period. 9/10 short-term and 10/20 long-term periods are particularly popular with analysts.

The lines are usually distinguished using different colours in charting applications although solid and dotted lines may be used for publications.

Buy and sell signals are indicated as follows:

> If the short-term moving average comes from **below** and **crosses above** the long-term moving average, then this is a **buy** signal if the price action is **above** the moving average cross-over point.
>
> If the short-term moving average comes from **above** and **crosses below** the long-term moving average, then this is a **sell** signal if the price action is **below** the moving average cross-over point.

The crossover is considered to be much more significant if both averages are moving in the same direction.

If both averages are moving up, then it is known as a **Golden Cross**. If both averages are moving down, then it is known as a **Death Cross**.

Simple Moving Averages
This is the type of moving average which has already been described. It is simply the arithmetic average of the number of data points in the selected period.

A SMA inherently lags behind the market price action and therefore any signals produced will inevitably lag behind the trend change that caused the moving average(s) to reverse direction. Though SMAs provide a simple analytical technique they are still used widely by technical analysts.

Buy/sell signals

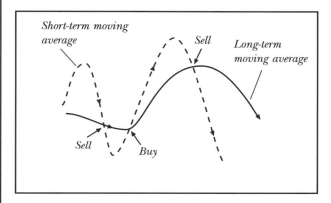

Simple Moving Average formula

$$SMA = \frac{P_1 + P_2 + P_3 + \ldots\ldots P_n}{n}$$

P = Price or value
n = Number of days in period

Moving Averages

Short-term SMAs are more responsive and more 'whippy' to price action than those for long-term averages. So what period should be used for moving averages? As has been mentioned already, analysts often use either the length of the trading cycle, or half its length. For example, in a 50-day futures market trading cycle the average period used is 50 or 25 days.

A SMA also assigns an **equal weight** to all the prices used to calculate the average. This approach disregards the importance and relevance of the most recent data as compared with the earlier data of the time series used to calculate the moving average. Something important may have happened very recently to affect the market which is not given sufficient weight. In order to overcome this and other deficiencies in the SMA, two other types of moving average can be used:

- Weighted Moving Average (WMA)
- Exponential Moving Average (EMA)

Both these averages are used in the same way as SMAs but differ in the way the average is calculated.

Weighted Moving Average
This technique uses a mathematical algorithm which assigns a **greater weight** or importance to the most recent data.

The example for a five day period illustrates the process. The price for each day is multiplied by its day number and added together. This total is divided by the sum of the day multipliers to determine the WMA. The older the day in the period the smaller the multiplier used.

Exponential Moving Average
This is similar to a WMA in that the average also assigns a greater weight to the most recent data. However, in this case, instead of using a fixed number of data points (the periodicity), the EMA uses **all** the data that is available. Each price entry becomes less significant but is still included in the calculation which uses a complicated formula.

Example of a Weighted Moving Average calculation

$$WMA = \frac{5 \times (P_1) + 4 \times (P_2) + 3 \times (P_3) + 2 \times (P_4) + 1 \times (P_5)}{(5 + 4 + 3 + 2 + 1) = 15}$$

P = Price or value, where P_1 is the most recent day and P_5 is the oldest day in the average.

Moving Averages

Bar chart of daily close prices for Bass PLC shares

Bar chart of daily close prices for Bass PLC shares

Bar chart of daily close prices for Bass PLC shares

Bar chart of daily close prices for Bass PLC shares

Relative Performance

Relative performance is a measure of how well an individual stock or stock market group of companies are performing relative to the market as a whole or relative to another stock, over a specified period.

If the relative performance is positive and rising, then the stock is outperforming the index. If the relative performance is falling, then this indicates underperformance.

As relative performance is a comparison, it is normal to plot the data at the bottom of a price chart as a sub-plot. The relative performance plots produced are used as indicators to detect and confirm market trends.

A change in trend of the relative performance chart may be a warning signal that something is changing in the share price itself. A move in a share price accompanied by a similar move in relative performance is taken as a reliable signal and confirmation to buy or sell.

Calculating Relative Strength

The formula to calculate relative strength for the closing price of a share against a stock index is as follows. (Note that the term relative strength is often used—rather than relative performance—with reference to the equity markets. Relative performance is the more common term for the FX, commodity and most future markets, as relative strength refers to Welles Wilder's RSI.)

$$\text{Relative strength} = \frac{\dfrac{A2}{B2} - \dfrac{A1}{B1}}{\dfrac{A1}{B1}}$$

A1 = Latest closing price for share
B1 = Latest closing price for stock index

A2 = Reference (start) closing price for share
B2 = Reference (start) closing price for stock index

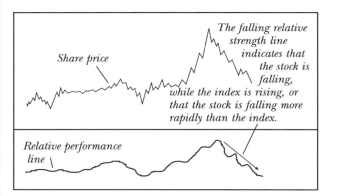

Share price

The falling relative strength line indicates that the stock is falling, while the index is rising, or that the stock is falling more rapidly than the index.

Relative performance line

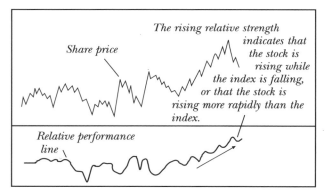

Share price

The rising relative strength indicates that the stock is rising while the index is falling, or that the stock is rising more rapidly than the index.

Relative performance line

Relative Performance

A line chart of daily closing prices for Bass PLC shares

Relative performance of Bass PLC shares compared with the FT-SE 100 Index over the same period

Relative strength in futures markets

Relative strength can also be used in futures markets. Examples are:

- Various commodities against the CRB (Commodity Research Board) Index
- Various substitutes against each other, eg, various grains against wheat
- Silver against gold (there is thought to be a long-established link between their prices)

This shows a line chart for daily last trade values for the Nikkei 225 Index and a bar chart for daily last trade S&P 500 Index values

The relative performance sub-chart shows that the S&P 500 starts to perform consistently better than the Nikkei from the middle of July

Gaps

If price action evolves such that no trading occurs between, for example, the close of one price and where it next opens, then a **gap** or hole is produced in a price chart. However, subsequent trading within the new period may succeed in filling this gap. A true gap means that there is no trading price overlap because the prices have skipped a price area. A gap occurs when the majority of market players simultaneously decide that prices should be adjusted swiftly. Thus a gap may be defined as follows:

> The **low** price of a period is **higher** than the high price of the preceeding period or conversely the **high** of the period is **lower** than the preceding low.

Gaps are commonly seen in futures markets, much less so in liquid equity markets and rarely in spot **FX** currency markets.

This reason for this is that futures are hedging instruments and traders are long or short at any given time. They may react quickly to unexpected events by placing orders that move the price dramatically and very quickly, causing a gap to appear.

Gaps are patterns which are used to determine and confirm price moves. There are four basic types of gaps which have different uses:

- Common
- Breakaway
- Runaway
- Exhaustion

Common Gap
This type is seen in a sideways or congestion trading area and usually indicates a market's lack of interest in the price of an instrument. This type of gap is also found typically with low volume trading where there are few active market participants.

Breakaway Gap
This type of gap usually occurs at the end of a consolidation such as an ascending triangle and signals the start of a significant market move. This type also usually occurs on a heavy volume of trading and is associated with a volume increase at the time of the gap.

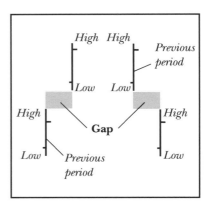

Common gap

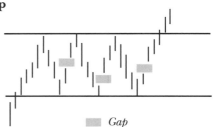

Breakaway gap

Gaps

Runaway Gap

This occurs typically in the middle of a price move and is used to estimate the size of a move – it is taken as a signal of a continuing trend. The volume may not increase at the gap but if it does, then it usually indicates a strong trend. The runaway gap is also sometimes called a **measuring** gap, because it occurs halfway up a trend (in reality this seldom occurs) and a **continuation** gap, because it indicates continuation of the trend.

As the gap usually occurs in the middle of a price move the final price move is easily calculated using the price difference from the beginning of the move to the gap.

Exhaustion Gap

This type signals the end of a price move and can be confused with a runaway gap. Typically an exhaustion gap occurs very near to the last day of a price trend which then reverses. The difference between an exhaustion and a runaway gap is that the former involves a very high volume of trading.

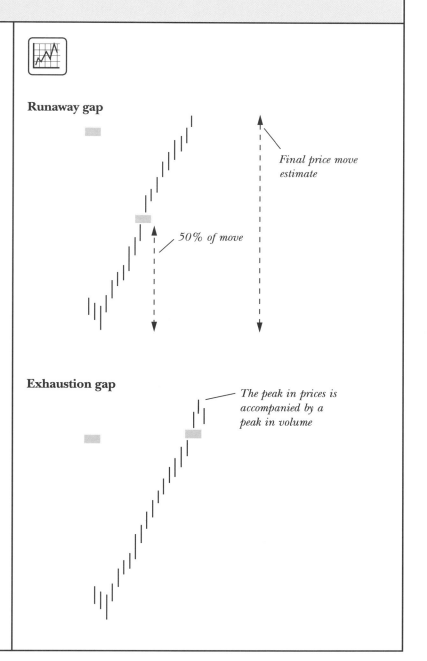

Runaway gap

Final price move estimate

50% of move

Exhaustion gap

The peak in prices is accompanied by a peak in volume

Gaps

A bar chart of daily last trade prices for 3 month forward contracts for Nickel on the LME

Labels on chart: *Common*, *Common (long-term) or breakaway (short-term)*, *Breakaway (long-term) or runaway (short-term)*, *Breakaway*

○ *Some of the more obvious gaps are within the highlighted areas*

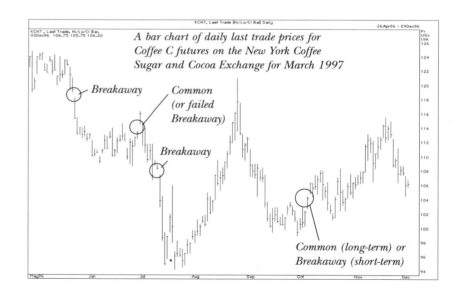

A bar chart of daily last trade prices for Coffee C futures on the New York Coffee Sugar and Cocoa Exchange for March 1997

Labels on chart: *Breakaway*, *Common (or failed Breakaway)*, *Breakaway*, *Common (long-term) or Breakaway (short-term)*

Charting Examples

This screen is from Reuters and shows Relative Performance for
Cadbury shares, relative to the FT All Share index and to the FTFM
index, which is the appropriate FT market sector for Food
Processing.

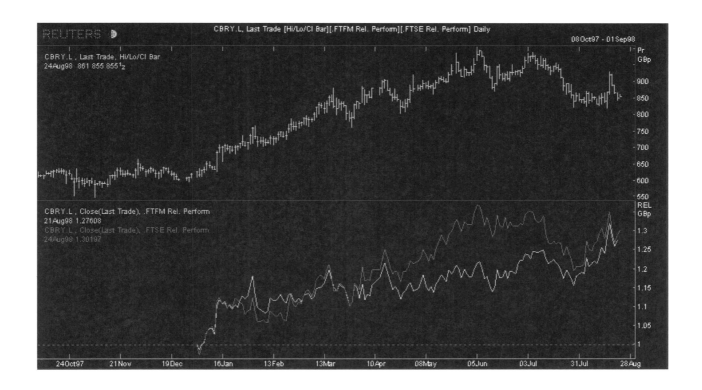

The screens are meant to show you what additional information about Cadbury you could gather if you were using Reuters Graphic services. They show a 2 year daily bar chart for Cadbury shares.

The first chart is an example of the Moving Average simple option with an average period of 100 days.

The second chart has a 14-day Weighted Moving Average and a 21-day Exponential Moving Average added to it.

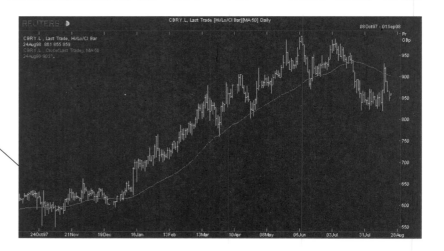

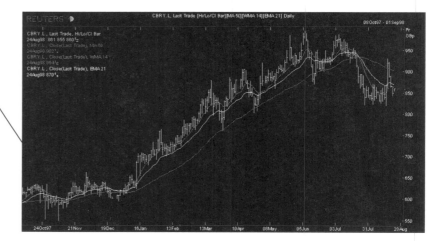

Summary

You have now finished the third section of the book and you should have a clear understanding of the following patterns:

- Trendlines

- Continuation/consolidation patterns

- Reversal patterns

- Support and resistance

- Moving averages

- Relative performance

- Gaps

As a check on your understanding of this section you should try the Quick Quiz Questions. You may also find the Overview section to be a helpful learning tool.

Quick Quiz Questions

1. This chart has a number of patterns. Indicate and name as many as you can.

2. This chart has a wedge pattern. Indicate its position.

You can check your answers on page 92.

Overview

Trendlines

- Line connecting consecutive high or low data points in order to identify the **direction** of a market
- **Uptrend** is a line connecting at least 3 consecutive rising low points and is drawn **under** the points
- **Downtrend** is a line connecting at least 3 consecutive falling high points and is drawn **above** the points

Support and Resistance Lines

- **Support line** – level that supports market price action for a period of time
- **Resistance line** – level that resists market price action for a period of time
- **Retracement**– as a market reacts following a strongly trending move, part of the price move is retraced

Continuation/Consolidation Patterns

- Occur during consolidation where prices are moving **sideways** rather than in an up or down trend
- Most common continuation patterns are:
  - **Triangles**
  - **Rectangles**
  - **Flags and pennants**

Relative Performance

- Measure of how well an individual stock or group of stocks are performing **relative** to the market as a whole, or relative to another stock, over a specified period

Patterns

Reversal Patterns

- Indicate an impending **top** or **bottom** in market prices coupled with a **trend reversal**
- Patterns that signal the end of a down trend are the inverse of those that signal the end of an uptrend
- Most common reversal patterns are:
  - **Head and Shoulders**
  - **Double and Triple tops/bottoms**
  - **Wedges**
  - **Rounding or Saucer top/bottoms**

Moving Averages

- A moving average is created by adding a series of closing prices and dividing by a particular number of periods. For simple moving averages, the price is averaged over a number of days. On each successive day the oldest price drops out of the average and is replaced by the current price - hence the average moves daily. Exponential and weighted moving averages use the same technique but weight the figures - least weight to the oldest price, most to the current price
- **Simple Moving Average** (SMA) is a simple arithmetic average in the selected period
- **Weighted Moving Average** (WMA) assigns a greater weight to more recent prices
- **Exponential Moving Average** (EMA) assigns a greater weight to more recent prices but uses all the prices – the oldest price is not dropped off

Gaps

- A gap occurs when there has been no trading between two consecutive price bars
- There are four types:
  - **Common**
  - **Breakaway**
  - **Runaway or measuring**
  - **Exhaustion**

Further Resources

Books

Technical Analysis of the Futures Markets
John J. Murphy, New York Institute of Finance, 1986
ISBN   0 13 898008 X

Technical Analysis Explained
Martin Pring, McGraw-Hill, 1991
ISBN   0 0705 1042 3

The New Commodity Trading Systems and Methods
Perry Kaufman, J. Wiley & Sons, 1987
ISBN   0 4718 7879 0

Technical Analysis from A – X
Steven Achelis, Probus Publishing Co., 1995
ISBN   1 55738 816 4

Technical Analysis of Stock Trends Chapter 2
Robert D. Edwards and John Magee, John Magee Inc
ISBN   0 910944 00 8

Technical Analysis of Stocks and Commodities

Reversal Patterns by M.F. Bowman
Vol. 8:10 (371-376), 1990

Consolidation Patterns by M.F. Bowman and T. Hartle
Vol. 8:11 (405-409), 1990

Gaps by T. Hartle and M.F. Bowman
Vol. 8:12 (453-455), 1990

Calculating Relative Strength of Stocks by R. L. Hand
Vol. 10:5 (235-237), 1992

Support and Resistance Levels by J.J. Kosar
Vol. 11:1 (17-19), 1993

Trade with Moving Averages by C. Alexander
Vol. 11:6 (257-260), 1993

RFT Web Site at http://www.wiley-rft.reuters.com
This is the series' companion web site where additional quiz
questions, updated screens and other information may be found.

Quick Quiz Answers

1. *This chart has a number of patterns. Indicate and name as many as you can.*

2. *This chart has a wedge pattern. Indicate its position.*

This section of the book should take about 60 minutes of study time. You may not take as long as this or you may take a little longer – remember your learning is individual to you.

In 1954, I was fortunate to join Investment Educators as a 'gopher'. I carried luggage, ran the projector, made charts and took attendance for the owner, Ralph Dystant, and for the technical 'guru', Roy Larson.

Lane's Stochastics by George G. Lane MD
Technical Analysis of Stocks and Commodities, Vol. 2:3 (87-90), 1984

Introduction

The construction of charts is relatively straightforward, but as you have seen, the process of identifying patterns is much more complicated. The patterns seen in charts are seldom exact text-book versions of ones you are seeking. The result is that predictions based on price movement charts exclusively are never completely reliable.

What can market players do to improve the reliability of their predictions of future market trends? What kind of tools and techniques are available? You will probably remember that even Dow recognised that he needed confirmation of a trend before implementing any particular trading strategy. Dow used volume as one of his indicators.

Confirmation when:
Increasing volume on
uptrend highs and
decreasing volume on
uptrend lows – opposite
for downtrend

Volume
data

Market players use a variety of **indicators** to confirm or reinforce their trading strategies which they have derived from charting. Many indicators are now in use; some are easy to use and others involve complex mathematical calculations which have been developed by market practitioners. It is important to recognise that different indicators can be better suited to different types of market instruments, for example, equities and spot FX currencies. Successful analysts use a 'cocktail' of indicators to derive a trading strategy – it would be a mistake to use a single indicator in isolation. Indicators which are used in fast- moving commodities futures markets will not necessarily be so successful in the more long- term equities markets or those used for stock indices. It is also worth noting that as the power of computing techniques is constantly being improved and as markets are expanded, so too are the numbers of indicators – either new or adaptations of existing techniques.

In most cases indicators are plotted on sub-charts using the vertical axis for the indicator and the horizontal axis for time. These indicator plots are usually placed beneath the price movement plot so that both plots use the same time axis. The chart below shows a typical combination of price movement and volume charts for an equity.

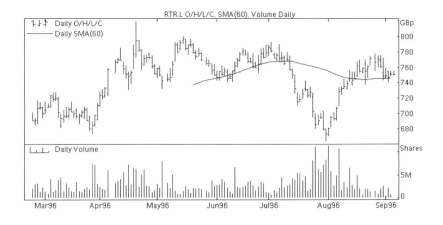

Types of Indicators

There are two basic types of indicators you will encounter:

- **Confirmation** or **divergence indicators**
  As their name implies, confirmation indicators confirm underlying **trends.** Divergence is when the indicator line moves away from the price line in an opposite direction. In effect, divergence is non-confirmation, which is seen as a warning signal.

- **Momentum indicators** or **oscillators**
  These indicators measure the rate of change, or velocity, of price movements as opposed to the actual price levels and are used to help determine a **trading strategy**. Divergence is also a very important factor in utilising these indicators.

Indicators

Confirmation or Divergence Indicators

These indicators are based on, or associated with, the primary price movement chart. You have already been introduced to most of these indicators either in the *Chart Types* or *Patterns* sections and they include:

- Volume
- Open interest
- Relative performance
- Moving averages

Volume	This is one of the oldest indicators – orginally used by Dow. The values are obtained from separate data associated with the instrument prices. Generally volume is used to confirm price movement – divergence is taken as a warning signal.

Open interest	This is similar to volume in use. The values are also obtained from separate data associated with the instrument prices. Futures traders use this indicator – a strong trend should be confirmed by rising open interest.

Relative performance	Relative performance measures the relationship between a particular instrument and the overall performance of the market or market sector. Any rises or falls must be put in context – for example, a share price rise of 15% is not impressive if the average market sector rise is 25%. A change in the relative performance trend can indicate an impending change in the underlying price trend.

Moving average	Moving averages are used to smooth price information in order to confirm trends and support and resistance levels. They are also useful in deciding on a trading strategy particularly in futures trading or a market with a strong up or down trend. For **simple moving averages** the price is averaged over a number of days. On each successive day the oldest price drops out of the average and is replaced by the current price – hence the average moves daily. **Exponential** and **weighted moving averages** use the same technique but weight the figures – least weight to the oldest price, most to the current price.

Momentum Indicators or Oscillators

These indicators measure the rate of change, or velocity, of directional price movement and are used to give warning of short-term turning points.

When prices move up rapidly they are said to be **overbought** and this is taken as a signal **not to buy**. When prices move down rapidly they are said to be **oversold** and the signal is **not to sell**. A heavily overbought/oversold situation is generally taken as an indication that a market reaction or possibly even a reversal is imminent. The reaction to a heavily overbought market can be a period of sideways consolidation. Oscillators include:

- Relative Strength Index (RSI)
- Stochastic Oscillator
- Moving Average Convergence Divergence (MACD)

Relative Strength Index (RSI)

This index was created by the US analyst J. Welles Wilder, Jr. and is a popular indicator which is applied to FX, commodity, equity and commodity or financial futures markets. The indicator compares an instrument only with its **own** past performance.

The RSI measures the ratio of up-moves to down-moves and normalises the calculation so that the index is expressed in a range 0 – 100. If the RSI is 70 or greater then the instrument is seen as overbought – a situation whereby prices have risen more than market expectations. An RSI of 30 or less is taken as a signal that the instrument may be oversold – a situation whereby prices have fallen more than market expectations. Many analysts prefer to use overbought/oversold levels of 80/20 rather than 70/30.

Stochastic Oscillator

This is used to indicate overbought/oversold conditions on a scale 0 – 100%. The indicator is based on the observation that in a a strong up trend, closing prices for periods tend to concentrate in the higher part of the period's range. Conversely, as prices fall in a strong down trend, closing prices tend to be near to the extreme low of the period range.

Stochastic calculations produce two lines, %K and %D which are used to indicate overbought/oversold areas on a chart. Divergence between the stochastic lines and the price action of the underlying instrument gives a powerful trading signal.

Moving Average Convergence Divergence (MACD)

This indicator was devised by Gerald Appel and involves plotting two momentum lines. The **MACD line** is the difference between two exponential moving averages and the **signal** or **trigger** line which is an exponential moving average of the difference. If the MACD and trigger lines cross, then this is taken as a signal that a change in trend is likely.

Volume, Open Interest, Relative Performance and Moving Average as chart types or patterns have already been discussed but examples of their use as indicators are covered in this section.

Momentum indicators are described using the same format as used in previous sections and cover:

- Relative Strength Index (RSI)
- Stochastic Oscillator
- Moving Average Convergence Divergence (MACD)

It is important to remember that this book is not an exhaustive treatment of indicators – it only provides an overview of the subject. If you want to find out more then you might like to have a look at some of the materials given in **Further Resources**.

Relative Strength Index

J. Welles Wilder, Jr. originally developed the **Relative Strength Index** indicator for use with price bar charts of individual stocks, commodities or stock indices. However, the RSI is now used in all markets. The indicator compares an instrument only with its **own past performance.** It is not a comparison with other instruments or the market in general – this is Relative performance.

The RSI should be used in conjunction with price movement charts but not together with other indicators of the same type, for example, stochastics. RSI values lie in the range 0 – 100 which may be used to indicate the following:

❏ **Overbought/oversold** conditions

A line is drawn at 70/80 above which the instrument is said conventionally to be overbought and is a signal to exercise caution in buying at that level. Below a line at 30/20 the instrument is said to be oversold and it is a signal to think carefully before selling.

❏ **Tops** and **bottoms**
A top may be signified when a RSI peak is seen through the 80/70 level followed by a down-turn; similarly a bottom may be signified by a RSI trough through the 30/20 level followed by an up-turn. The RSI analysis provides only part of the evidence needed for market confidence that a top/bottom has been formed.

❏ **Patterns**
Typical patterns such as head and shoulders, tops/bottoms and pennants may be more obvious in the RSI chart than in the price chart.

❏ **Divergence**
Divergence between price action and RSI is often taken as a strong indication of a market turning point. Thus in an uptrend, price action makes new highs compared with the previous peak but the RSI indicator fails to reach and surpass its equivalent previous high point.

Calculating the Index

The RSI measures the ratio of average prices and normalises the calculations so the index values lie between 0 and 100. The index may be calculated using the following basic algorithm:

$$RSI = 100 - \left[\frac{100}{1 + RS} \right]$$

Where:

$$RS = \frac{\text{Sum of the 'up closes' in } n \text{ days'}}{\text{Sum of the 'down closes' in the same } n \text{ days'}}$$

Up close is the **price change** between consecutive periods where the close has moved higher
Down close is the **price change** between consecutive periods where the close has moved lower

Wilder originally used n = 14 but other periods in common use are 9 and 21 days.

The more conventional formula to calculate RSI looks similar to the algorithm above but uses Exponential Moving Averages, which serve to smooth the resultant line, and is calculatedd as follows:

$$RS = \frac{\text{Average of the 'up closes' in } n \text{ days'}}{\text{Average of the 'down closes' in the same } n \text{ days'}}$$

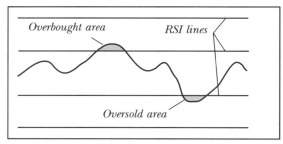

One technique is to vary the level of the overbought/oversold lines according to whether the market is in up or down trend. For example, in an uptrending chart the lines may be drawn at 80 and 40, whereas in a downtrending chart they may be drawn at 60 and 20.

Relative Strength Index

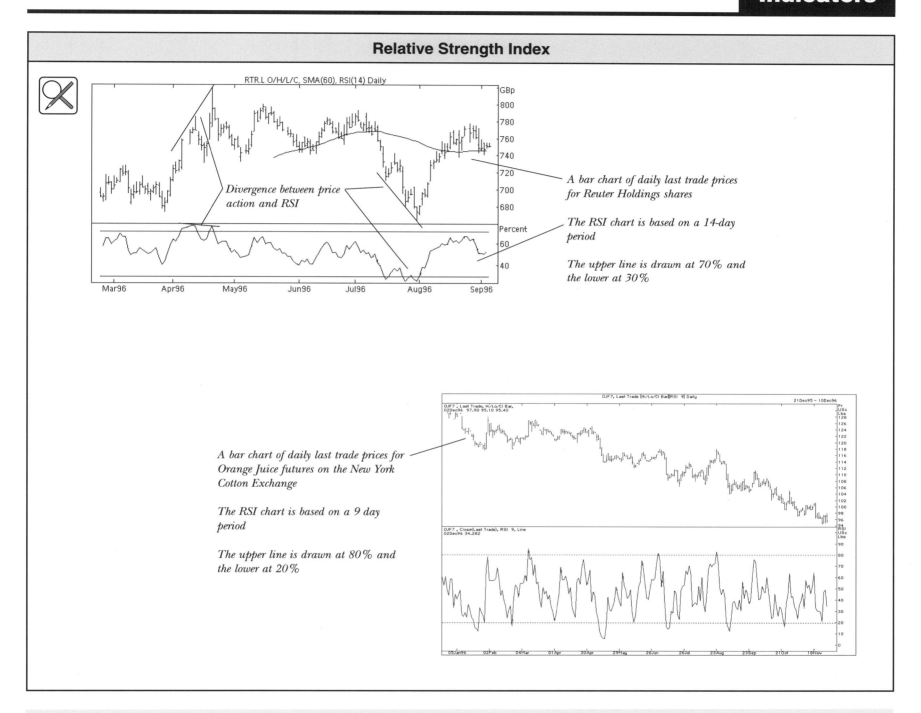

RTR.L O/H/L/C, SMA(60), RSI(14) Daily

A bar chart of daily last trade prices for Reuter Holdings shares

Divergence between price action and RSI

The RSI chart is based on a 14-day period

The upper line is drawn at 70% and the lower at 30%

A bar chart of daily last trade prices for Orange Juice futures on the New York Cotton Exchange

The RSI chart is based on a 9 day period

The upper line is drawn at 80% and the lower at 20%

Stochastic Oscillators

Stochastic oscillators originated as an engineering analytical technique and were adapted by the US analyst George C Lane as a way of indicating overbought/oversold conditions using a simple % scale. A key use of the indicator is to look for divergence between the stochastic lines and that of the instrument price itself. This information can be used to reinforce buy/sell trading decisions.

Stochastics are based on observations of instrument prices:

- As prices **decrease** in a trending market, the **closes** tend to be nearer the extreme **lows** of the period price range

- As prices **increase** in a trending market, the **closes** tend to be nearer the extreme **highs** of the period price range

The stochastic analysis is available in two forms – **fast** and **slow**. **Fast** stochastics use two **oscillating lines** which are shown as different colours in charting applications or as solid or broken lines in publications. The **raw value** or **%K line** (solid line) is shown on a chart scale 0 – 100. The other line, shown on the same chart, is a simple **moving average** of %K and is called the **%D line** (broken line).

Slow stochastics use the %D line of fast stochastics together with a simple moving average of this line – usually called the **Slow D**. Fast stochastics give a strongly oscillating chart and it is for this reason that many analysts prefer now to use slow stochastics.

As for the RSI indicator, stochastics are used to identify potentially overbought/oversold situations. Divergence between the stochastics' performance and that of the underlying price action is very important.

Overbought conditions are generally taken as occurring when the lines move **over 70/80%**; **oversold** is taken when the lines move **below 30/20%**.

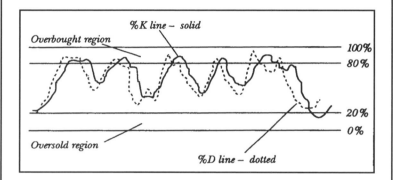

Stochastic Oscillators

The fact that a market is indicated as overbought should not be seen necessarily as a sell signal or indication of an imminent trend reversal. In any strongly trending market, overbought/oversold conditions can exist for a considerable perod of time. One of the most powerful signals that stochastics can deliver is that of divergence. However, the key to the successful use of stochastics is to use them in association with other indicators/analyses to indicate when a market is grossly overbought/oversold.

Calculations

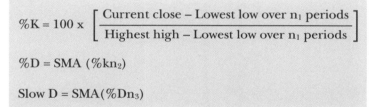

$$\%K = 100 \times \left[\frac{\text{Current close} - \text{Lowest low over } n_1 \text{ periods}}{\text{Highest high} - \text{Lowest low over } n_1 \text{ periods}} \right]$$

$$\%D = \text{SMA } (\%kn_2)$$

$$\text{Slow D} = \text{SMA}(\%Dn_3)$$

By far the most common value used for n2 is 3. Thus for fast stochastics, %D is the 3 period simple moving average of %K. For slow stochastics, almost without exception, the value for n3 is 3. Thus Slow D is the 3 period simple moving average of %D.

Bearish Divergence

This is indicated when %D forms **two** peaks, the second lower than the first, in the **overbought** region, while the underlying prices are rising. Confirmation to **sell** comes when, for Slow stochastics, the %D line comes from **above** and crosses **below** the Slow D line.

Bullish Divergence

This is indicated when %D forms **two** troughs, the second higher than the first, in the **oversold** region, while the underlying prices are falling. Confirmation to **buy** comes when for Slow stochastics, the %D line comes from **below** and crosses **above** the Slow D line.

Bearish Divergence

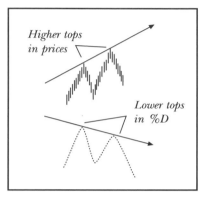

Higher tops in prices

Lower tops in %D

Bullish Divergence

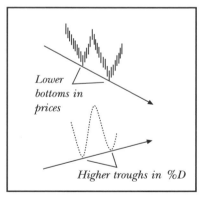

Lower bottoms in prices

Higher troughs in %D

Stochastic Oscillators

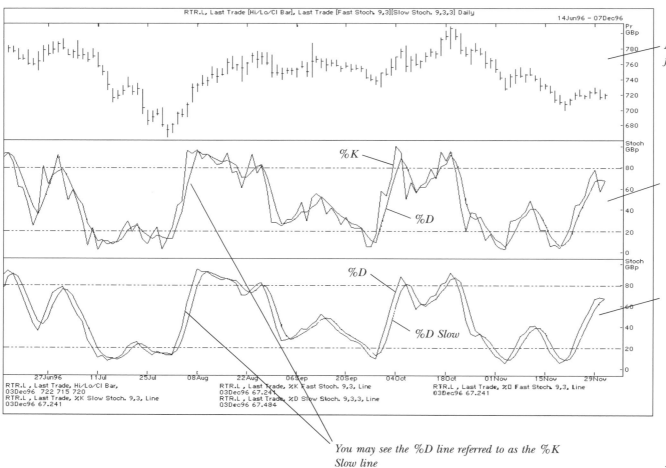

A bar chart of daily prices for Reuter Holdings shares

The middle section shows the **Fast stochastic** %D (9,3) and %K (9) lines, which are shown in different colours onscreen – the overbought and oversold lines are shown at 80% and 20% respectively

The lower section shows the **Slow stochastic** %D Slow (9,3,3) and %D (9,3) lines, which are shown in different colours onscreen – the overbought and oversold lines are shown at 80% and 20% respectively

The first of the figures shown in brackets relating to %D and %K indicate the length of period used. The second and third figures represent the moving average for the number of periods used

You may see the %D line referred to as the %K Slow line

Stochastic Oscillators

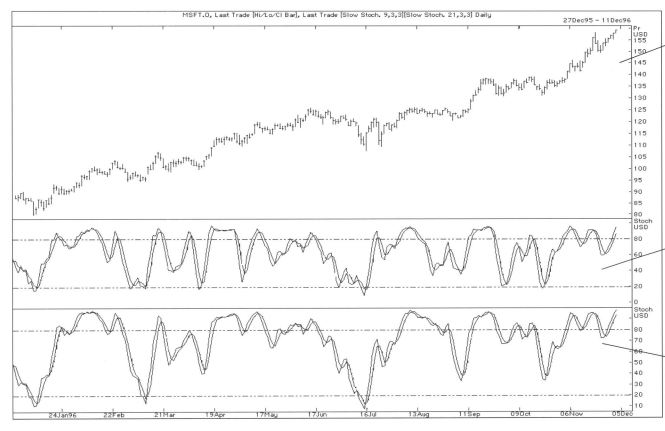

MSFT.O, Last Trade [Hi/Lo/Cl Bar], Last Trade [Slow Stoch. 9,3,3][Slow Stoch. 21,3,3] Daily   27Dec95 - 11Dec96

A bar chart of daily last trade prices for Microsoft shares

The middle section shows the Slow stochastic %D Slow (9,3,3) and %D (9,3) lines, which are shown in different colours onscreen – the overbought and oversold lines are shown at 80% and 20% respectively

The lower section shows the Slow stochastic %D Slow (21,3,3) and %D (21,3) lines, which are shown in different colours onscreen – the overbought and oversold lines are shown at 80% and 20% respectively

The first of the figures shown in brackets relating to %D and %K indicate the length of period used. The second and third figures represent the moving average for the number of periods used

Moving Average Convergence Divergence

The **Moving Average Convergence Divergence (MACD)** oscillator indicator was devised by Gerald Appel as a technique to signal trend changes and indicate trend direction. It was originally designed to observe the stock market's 26- and 13-week cycles. The procedure uses two exponential moving average lines to indicate overbought/oversold signals that oscillate above and below a zero line. There are no upper or lower boundaries, for example 0 - 100, as used in stochastics or the RSI.

First Line

This is usually displayed as a solid line and is called the **Fast MACD line** or plot. This line is the difference between a short and long moving average of the price — usually with smoothing factors equivalent to 12/13 and 26 period EMAs being used.

Second Line

This is often displayed as a dotted line, or a line of different colour in charting applications, and is called the **Slow MACD** or **signal** line. This line is an exponential moving average of the Fast MACD line. It is usual to see a smoothing factor equivalent to 9 periods used in the EMA. Gerald Appel recommended 9, 12 and 26 as the periods which should be used for the MACD lines.

In common with moving averages, MACD is used to determine buy/sell signals and to detect trend changes.

Sell Signal

This is indicated when the Fast MACD line crosses from **above to below** the signal line when both have positive values. The higher **above** the zero line this crossover occurs, the stronger the signal is said to be. Crossovers which occur with negative values should be ignored.

Buy Signal

This is indicated when the Fast MACD line crosses from **below to above** the signal line when both have negative values. The further **below** the zero line this crossover occurs, the stronger the signal is said to be.

Sell signal

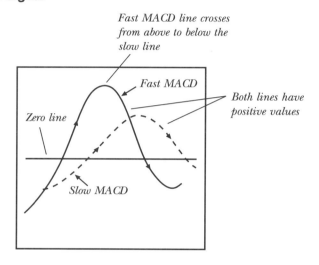

Fast MACD line crosses from above to below the slow line

Fast MACD

Both lines have positive values

Zero line

Slow MACD

Buy signal

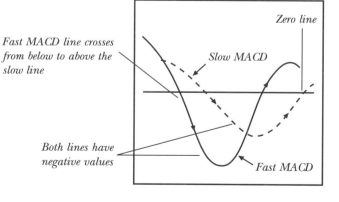

Zero line

Fast MACD line crosses from below to above the slow line

Slow MACD

Both lines have negative values

Fast MACD

Moving Average Convergence Divergence

Rather than plotting the analysis as two lines, a further technique is to plot the **difference** between the lines as a **forest line**, or linked **forest line graph**. This technique is very important as it is used to look for any divergence which may occur between the price action for the instrument and the MACD forest graph.

Fast MACD Line

Traditionally this is produced by subtracting a 26 equivalent period EMA from that for the 13 equivalent period EMA.

Slow MACD Line

This is formed by smoothing the fast line with a 9 equivalent period EMA.

Trends

Successive highest highs (or lowest lows) of market prices are compared with highest highs (or lowest lows) of MACD when plotted in forest graph form. If there is a divergence in trend between price action of the instrument and that of the MACD forest graph then this is taken as a good indicator of a possible trend reversal.

The criticisms of the MACD indicator are the same as those applied to moving averages in general – the most significant being that they lag the market.

Smoothing Factors

There is a simple formula which gives a good approximation between the smoothing factor used in the EMA algorithm and the equivalent number of periods (n):

$$\text{Smoothing factor} = \frac{2}{n + 1}$$

Smoothing factor	n
0.20	9
0.15	12
0.075	26

Buy/sell signals

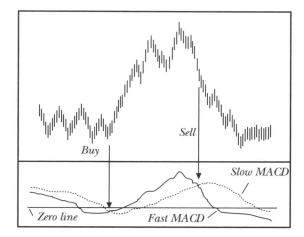

Divergence

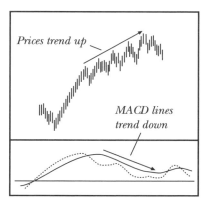

Moving Average Convergence Divergence

DEMFRF=, Bid [Candle][MACD 13,26,9][MACD Forest 13,26,9] Daily
25Apr96 – 09Dec96

DEMFRF=, Bid, Candle,
03Dec96 3.3800 3.3800 3.3789 3.3791

A candlestick chart of daily bid prices for DEM/FRF cross rates

DEMFRF=, Close(Bid), MACD 13,26,9, Line
03Dec96 0.00121
DEMFRF=, Close(Bid), Signal 13,26, Line
03Dec96 0.00153

Signal line

Zero line

The Fast MACD and Slow MACD signal lines are shown in different colours onscreen

DEMFRF=, Close(Bid), MACD Forest 13,26,9, Forest
03Dec96 0.0003

A forest graph showing the difference between the two MACD lines

22May96 19Jun 17Jul 14Aug 11Sep 09Oct 06Nov 04Dec

Moving Average Convergence Divergence

2EDH7, Last Trade [Hi/Lo/Cl Bar][MACD 13,26,9][MACD Forest 13,26,9] Daily

28Dec95 – 11Dec96   FREEZE

A bar chart of daily last trade prices for Eurodollar futures for March 1997 on the CME

The Fast MACD and Slow MACD signal lines are shown in different colours onscreen

Signal line   Zero line

A forest graph showing the difference between the two MACD lines

2EDH7 , Last Trade, Hi/Lo/Cl Bar,
03Dec96 94.57 94.54 94.56
2EDH7 , Close(Last Trade), Signal 13,26, Line
03Dec96 0.05251

2EDH7 , Close(Last Trade), MACD 13,26,9, Line
03Dec96 0.05641
2EDH7 , Close(Last Trade), MACD Forest 13,26,9, Forest
03Dec96 0.00

Charting Examples

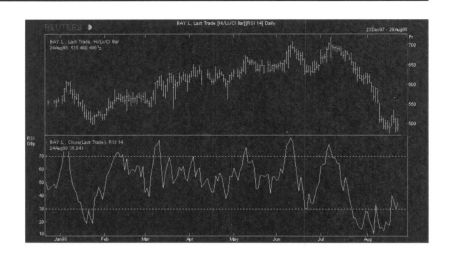

The screen on top right displays a daily bar chart for **British Airways** shares together with the Relative Strength Index indicator sub-chart for a 14-day period.

The screen on bottom right is the **Help** screen from the Reuters 3000 system. It displays useful information to help you see what the charts mean.

Stack:	Overlay:	Shows:	Upper left corner:
upper	1	bar chart with up to 2 years of daily open, high, low and close	date of last day plotted with open, high, low and close
	2	line chart with 60 day simple moving average of closing prices (or index values)	date of last day plotted with moving average price (or index value)
lower	1	line chart showing a 14-day RSI line. The scale of the chart is 0 to 100.	date of last day plotted with RSI value
	2	a horizontal upper boundary line through 70	
	3	a horizontal lower boundary line through 30	

Use the toolbar to modify the graph. Use the Edit button on the toolbar to open the Edit dialogue box to modify parameters. You can modify the moving average period for the upper graph and the RSI period, upper boundary and lower boundary for the lower graph.

The screen on top right displays a daily bar chart for **Reuters** shares over a year. The screen also displays the sub-charts for both **Fast** and **Slow** stochastics.

The screen on bottom right is the **Help** facility from the Reuters 3000 system. It displays further explanation on the sub-charts.

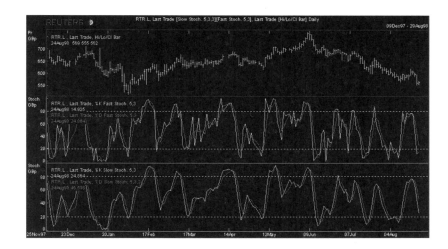

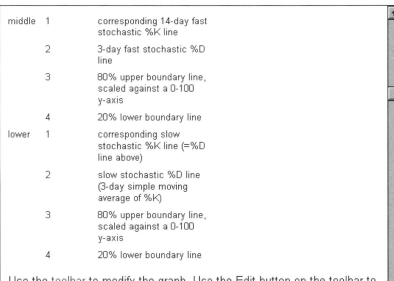

middle	1	corresponding 14-day fast stochastic %K line
	2	3-day fast stochastic %D line
	3	80% upper boundary line, scaled against a 0-100 y-axis
	4	20% lower boundary line
lower	1	corresponding slow stochastic %K line (=%D line above)
	2	slow stochastic %D line (3-day simple moving average of %K)
	3	80% upper boundary line, scaled against a 0-100 y-axis
	4	20% lower boundary line

Use the toolbar to modify the graph. Use the Edit button on the toolbar to open the Edit dialogue box to modify parameters. You can modify the moving average period for the upper graph and the RSI period, upper boundary and lower boundary for the lower graph.

The screen to the right shows a 1 year daily bar chart for **Cadbury** shares. The sub-chart below it displays the **Fast** and **Slow** MACD options.

The **fast** MACD line is line Ⓐ with the MACD W (Weighted) legend – the **slow** or signal MACD line is line Ⓑ with the MACD legend.

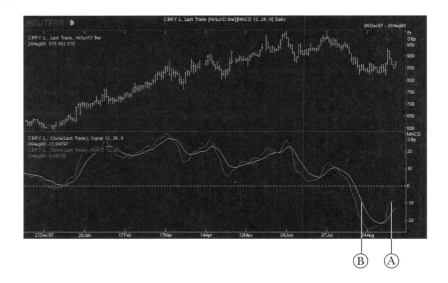

Summary

You have now finished the fourth section of the book and you should have a clear understanding of the following indicators:

- Relative Strength Index (RSI)

- Stochastic Oscillator

- Moving Average Convergence Divergence (MACD)

As a check on your understanding of this section you should try the Quick Quiz Questions. You may also find the Overview section to be a helpful learning tool.

Quick Quiz Questions

1. Which of the following statements are true and which are false concerning the Relative Strength Index indicator?

	True	False
a) The indicator compares an instrument with another instrument's past performance		
b) If the RSI chart line is over a line drawn at 80, the instrument is said to be overbought		
c) Divergence between price action and RSI is often an indication of a market turning point		
d) Patterns such as head and shoulders are not very obvious in an RSI chart		

2. The following diagram shows two sections, A & B, of a Stochastic %D line sub-chart. A & B are examples of Bullish and Bearish divergence, but which is which?

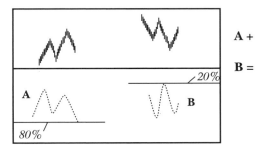

A +

B =

3. Complete the missing words in the following statement.

When using the MACD indicator a selling signal is indicatedwhen the Fast MACD line crosses from ☐ ☐ **to** ☐ the signal line when both have positive values. The further ☐ **above** the zero line this crossover occurs, the stronger the signal is said to be.

You can check your answers on page 114.

Overview

Relative Strength Index (RSI)

- Developed by **Welles Wilder, Jr.**, this indicator is applied to FX, commodity and equity markets

- Compares an instrument only with its **own** past performance

- **RSI values lie in the range 0 – 100:**

    Overbought line is usually set at 70/80

    Oversold line is usually set at 30/20

Indicators

Stochastic Oscillator

- Adopted by **Lane** as a way of indicating **overbought/oversold** conditions using a simple **% scale**

- Provides a way of signalling **divergence** between a stochastic line and instrument price

- Two types of stochastic analysis – **Fast** and **Slow**

- **Fast** stochastics uses two oscillating lines – the **raw value** or **%K line** and a simple moving average of %K line called the **%D line**

- **Slow** stochastics uses the **%D line** together with a simple moving average of this line called the **Slow D line**

- **Overbought conditions are usually over 70/80%**

- **Oversold conditions are usually under 30/20%**

Moving Average Convergence Divergence (MACD)

- Devised by **Appel** this oscillator signals **trend changes** and indicates **trend directions**

- **Fast MACD** line is the difference between a short and long moving average of the price

- **Slow MACD** or **signal** line is an exponential moving average of the Fast MACD line

- **Sell signal** – when the Fast MACD line crosses from **above to below** the signal line when both have **positive** values

- **Buy signal** – when the Fast MACD line crosses from **below to above** the signal line when both have **negative** values

Further Resources

Books

Technical Analysis of the Futures Markets
John J. Murphy, New York Institute of Finance, 1986
ISBN   0 13 898008 X

Technical Analysis Explained
Martin Pring, McGraw-Hill, 1991
ISBN   0 0705 1042 3

The New Commodity Trading Systems and Methods
Perry Kaufman, J. Wiley & Sons, 1987
ISBN   0 4718 7879 0

Technical Analysis from A – X
Steven Achelis, Probus Publishing Co., 1995
ISBN   1 55738 816 4

Martin Pring on Momentum
Martin J. Pring, International Institute for Economic Research Inc, 1993
ISBN   1 55738 508 4

Trading for a Living
Dr. Alexander Elder, J. Wiley & Sons, 1993
ISBN   0 471 59224 2

Computer Analysis of the Futures Market
Charles Le Beau & David W. Lucas, Business One Irwin, 1992
ISBN   1 55623 468 6

Schwager on Futures - Technical Analysis
Jack D. Schwager, J. Wiley & Sons, 1996
ISBN   0 471 02051 6

Technical Analysis of Stocks and Commodities

Lane's Stochastics by G.C. Lane
Vol. 2:3 (87-90), 1984

Stochastic oscillator by M. Takano
Vol. 7:3 (86-86), 1989

Stochastic Oscillator: Sidebar
Vol. 8:2 (469-472), 1990

Stochastics by T. Hartle
Vol. 9:3 (103-103), 1991

Stochastics Indicators and Trading by D. Lundgren
Vol. 11:3 (144-146), 1993

RSI Variations by B. Star
Vol. 11:7 (292-297), 1993

The MACD Momentum Oscillator by B. Star
Vol. 12:2 (81-85), 1994

Using Indicators in Trading Ranges and Trends by B.C. Kramer
Vol. 12:4 (153-157), 1994

RFT Web Site at http://www.wiley-rft.reuters.com
This is the series' companion web site where additional quiz questions, updated screens and other information may be found.

Quick Quiz Answers

Your notes

1. Which of the following statements are true and which are false concerning the Relative Strength Index indicator?

	True	False
a) The indicator comapres an instrument with another insrument's past performance		✔
b) If the RSI chart line is over a line drawn at 80, the instrument is said to be overbought	✔	
c) Divergence between price action and RSI is often an indication of a market turning point	✔	
d) Patterns such as head and shoulders are not very obvious in an RSI chart		✔

2. The following diagram shows two sections, A & B, of a Stochastic %D line sub-chart. A & B are examples of Bullish and Bearish divergence, but which is which?

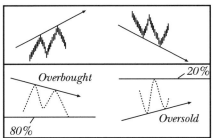

A = Bearish

B = Bullish

3. Complete the missing words in the following statement.

When using the MACD indicator a selling signal is indicated when the Fast MACD line crosses from │**above**│ to │**below**│ the signal line when both have positive values. The further │**above**│ the zero line this crossover occurs, the stronger the signal is said to be.

Waves, Numbers and Cycles – Contents

This section of the book should take about 60 minutes of study time. You may not take as long as this or you may take a little longer – remember your learning is individual to you.

Betting on a horse, that's gambling; betting you can make three spades, that's entertainment; betting that cotton will go up three points, that's business. See the difference?

Gann Lines and Angles by Robert Pardo
Technical Analysis of Stocks and Commodities, Vol. 3:5 (177-183), 1985

Introduction

So far, you have seen that trend lines combined with pattern recognition and a variety of indicators can be used to determine the direction of prices and to drive tactics within a trading strategy.

Dow identified trends in the market and thought of the various types as major – the tide, intermediate – waves, and minor – ripples.

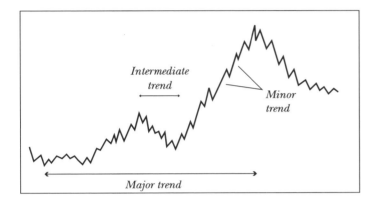

While recovering after an illness in 1927 a retired accountant, Ralph Nelson Elliott, spent time analysing the events in numerous Dow major trends. Like Dow, Elliott was interested in an overall perspective of market movements rather than how individual stocks performed.

In 1938, Elliott published his **Wave Theory**, which was devised to help explain why and where certain chart patterns develop and what they signalled. Elliott took Dow's original three phases of a bullish trend but considered the pattern to be closer to a repetitive rhythm of **five waves advancing** (bullish) and **three waves declining** (bearish). This rhythmic pattern was repeated over a wide range of time periods and was called a **cycle**.

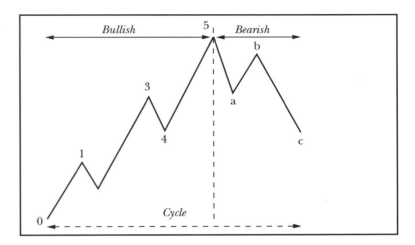

Elliott noticed that within cycles the same pattern was apparent – an advancing phase with peaks at 1,3 and 5, which he called **impulse waves** and troughs at 2 and 4, which he called **corrective waves**. Once the five-wave movement was complete the market moved into a three-wave corrective movement – a,b and c.

Elliott's Wave Theory has been applied to many markets now and has three important aspects.

- **Patterns**
  The most important element of the theory is that wave patterns exist which are repeated in cycles.

- **Time**
  Time relationships are used to confirm wave patterns. Elliott identified a number of time periods for cycles – the grand supercycle lasted 150 - 200 years whereas the sub-minuette lasted less than a day.

- **Ratio**
  Elliott noticed that there were 8 waves in some complete cycles; others had 34 and 144 waves. He also discovered there were mathematical relationships between the proportions of different waves.

Waves, Numbers and Cycles

What were these relationships and what was the significance of the ratios Elliott found? In measuring the proportions of peaks and troughs Elliott discovered that the ratio of wave height to the next

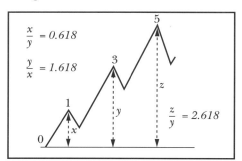

$\frac{x}{y} = 0.618$

$\frac{y}{x} = 1.618$

$\frac{z}{y} = 2.618$

higher wave was often, approximately **0.618** and the ratio to the previous **low** wave was approximately **1.618**. The ratio between **alternate** wave numbers was also consistently, approximately **2.618**. The reciprocal value of **1.618** is **0.618** and the reciprocal value of **2.618** is **0.382** which is another important number in Elliott Wave Theory.

What, if anything, did all these numbers mean? In the natural world there is a well established sequence of numbers governing events and phenomena such as plant leaf arrangements and the numbers of rabbits that can breed from a single pair. This sequence was first identified by an Italian mathematician in the thirteenth century – Leonardo Pisano or **Fibonacci**. Fibonacci identified the sequence as:

> **0, 1, 1, 2, 3, 5, 8, 13, 21, 34, 55, 89, 144,...**

The sequence is often referred to as **Fibonacci Numbers** and is easily calculated as each number in the sequence is obtained by summing the previous **two** digits. If you test these numbers, the further you move down the series, the truer the following statements:

- The ratio of any number to its **higher** number is **0.618**

- The ratio of any number to its **lower** number is **1.618**

- The ratio of **alternate** numbers is **2.618**

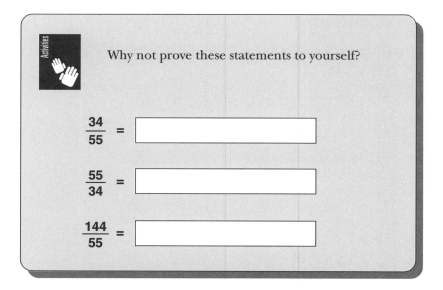

Why not prove these statements to yourself?

$\frac{34}{55} =$

$\frac{55}{34} =$

$\frac{144}{55} =$

The ratios of 0.618 and 1.618 were also known to ancient Greek and Eygptian scholars, artists and builders. The Golden Ratio, Section or Mean proportions were used in constructions such as the Great Pyramid of Giza and the Parthenon.

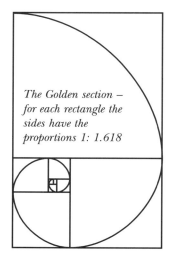

The Golden section – for each rectangle the sides have the proportions 1: 1.618

You will probably have noticed by now the striking similarity in the numbers associated with Elliott waves –

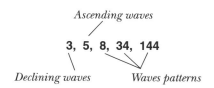

Ascending waves

3, 5, 8, 34, 144

Declining waves   *Waves patterns*

and wave ratios with Fibonacci numbers.

A different use of numbers and geometry was devised by William D. Gann who was a stock and commodity trader working in the first half of this century. Gann noticed that for particular stocks price movements of 25%, 50% and 100% were quite common – price moves of 33.33% and 66.67% ocurred but less frequently. So price rises and falls tended to follow ratios of 1, 2/3, 1/2, 1/3, and 1/4.

Gann also noted that there was a relationship between the **extent** of a price movement and the **time** the price took to reach its new level. If a share price moves one unit of price per one unit of time this results in a trendline of 45°. Gann described this as a **1 x 1** relationship or **squaring** of price and time.

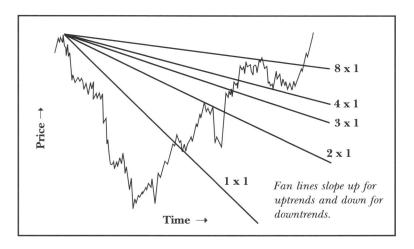

Fan lines slope up for uptrends and down for downtrends.

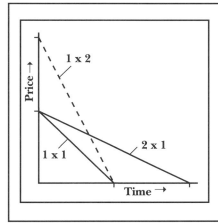

Not all charts use the same scales for prices and time so a 1 x 1 line will not necessarily be drawn at 45°.

The first number indicates time units – the second price units. So 2 x 1 means a line for two units of time/1 price unit and 1 x 2 represents one unit of time/2 price units.

Gann reasoned that if the price breaks through the trendline, the new trendline will have a mathematical relationship with the original one. For example, it could be 2x, 3x or 4x the price or it could be 1/2, 1/3, or 1/4 of the original.

A Gann chart uses a series of parallel horizontal lines which act as price targets together with a series of trendlines which **fan** out at the various Gann ratios from the start of a trend.

During his career Gann also produced many other tools and techniques such as 'trading rules' to help chartists and traders.

Most of the charts you have seen so far involve relatively short time periods. However, an investigation of price movements and market behaviour over much longer periods reveals some interesting **cycles** in stock market performance and individual price movements.

Edward R. Dewey noted that 18.2, 9.2 and 4 year cycle periods are important in stock markets – he also found that international battles follow a 22.2 year cycle!

In the 1920s, a Russian economist Nickolai D Kondratieff studied commodity prices, interest rates, wage levels and production indices in the US, UK, France and Germany. He concluded that there was a cycle of market behaviour repeating itself approximately every 54 years – quite close to the Fibonacci number 55.

The Kondratieff Wave

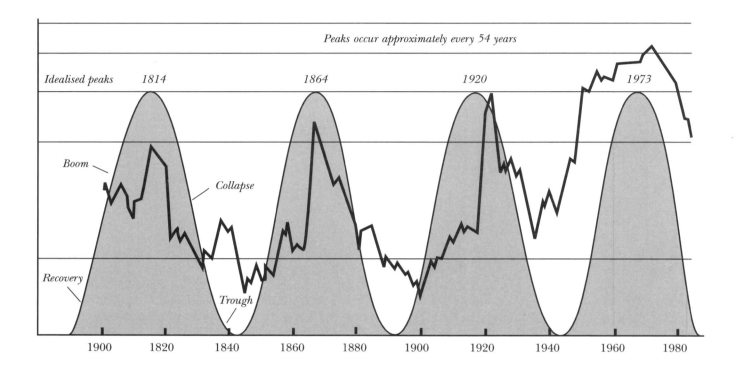

Peaks occur approximately every 54 years

Idealised peaks 1814   1864   1920   1973

Boom

Collapse

Recovery

Trough

1900   1820   1840   1860   1880   1900   1920   1940   1960   1980

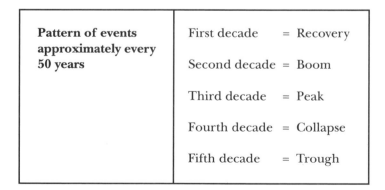

Pattern of events approximately every 50 years		
	First decade	= Recovery
	Second decade	= Boom
	Third decade	= Peak
	Fourth decade	= Collapse
	Fifth decade	= Trough

The wave and pattern theories that have been described so far are all based on **linear dynamics** – the patterns are based on orderly, recognisable and rhythmic patterns. However, as you may already know, market behaviour is not always so predictable and dramatic deviations from patterns occur – the stock market crash of 1987 is a good example.

More recently some mathematicians have shown that there is a correlation between price behaviour in the market place and the new science of **non-linear dynamic** – sometimes termed **Chaos Theory**. Non-linearity is simply explained as 'the effect is not proportional to the cause', as is the case in linear dynamics. A classic and well known saying describing the situation is 'It is the last straw that breaks the camel's back'. In a linear system if you throw a ball into the air with a certain force and at a certain trajectory you would be able to predict, accurately where the ball would land. In non-linear dynamics, although you know the ball will travel in a curve shape this time when you throw the ball you would not be able to predict accurately its trajectory or where it would land.

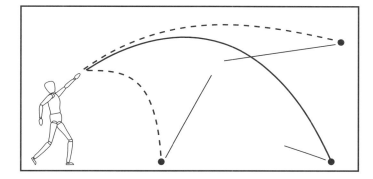

Non-linear systems require the massive computational power of a computer to produce a solution as to the relationship between cause and effect with any speed. Currently only those relationships that are slightly non-linear can be solved and be of use for forecasting markets – highly non-linear systems still lie outside the reach of present computing power.

One of the foundations of Chaos Theory is **fractal geometry** – objects that are fractals are similarly shaped however closely you examine them. There are many good examples of fractal patterns in nature,

for instance, looking at the branches of a tree at a distance and then looking closely at the twigs on one of the branches. The fractal nature of a freely trading market can be demonstrated through the observation that a weekly chart looks very much the same as those of daily, hourly, 5-minute etc charts. A fractal object is one that occupies a non-whole number set of dimensions. What does this mean? A flat piece of paper is two-dimensional but crumple it into a ball and it is now neither solid – three-dimensional – nor flat but somewhere in between. Mathematicians have shown that in some markets prices can be shown to be performing as fractals and thus Chaos Theory can be applied potentially in explaining market behaviour. But how can Chaos Theory help the trader if it cannot predict the future?

It is not necessary to be able to predict the future precisely in order to be able to make a trading profit. What is important is the ability to be able to predict shapes, patterns, trends in trading – Chaos Theory recognises shapes but not their precise size and movement.

Neither wave, cycle nor chaos theories completely explain all events in all markets. You have the choice now of selecting the tools and techniques you want to use to help determine your trading strategy for the markets you are involved with. It is well recognised that a successful strategy is made up of different techniques, for example, a combination of bar charts together with trend analysis and Bollinger bands.

You could toss a coin to decide whether to buy or sell in the market place but then there is no guarantee that you would get an accurate answer – the coin could be double-headed or someone else could grab the coin in mid-air or it may land on its rim and roll off the table and be lost....Even if your coin does land properly then, at best, over a period of time you will break-even using this technique. However, experience shows you will probably be a net loser! One of the greatest problems facing a trader is to learn when to take profits from a successful trade and when to exit a trade which is going wrong.

Waves, numbers and cycles are described using the same format as used in previous sections and cover:

- Elliott Wave Theory and Fibonacci numbers
- Gann Charts

Elliott Wave Theory and Fibonacci Numbers

The **Elliott Wave Theory** was devised by Ralph N. Elliott and has as its underlying principle the assumption that markets move in a **five wave pattern** in the direction of the trend, followed by a **three wave pattern** in the counter direction.

Elliott based his original work on stock market indices, for which it is still used successfully to classify and forecast market movements. Elliott Wave techniques do not work well for individual stocks though the techniques are used successfully for heavily traded instruments in a liquid market place, for example, spot FX, gold and actively traded futures. The techniques are not so successful for thinly traded instruments.

Patterns

These refer to the basic wave shapes which are repeated in **cycles**. Depending on the magnitude of the cycle, each complete set of waves can be **expanded** or **subdivided** into further sets of 5 and 3 waves. The number of waves resulting always follows the **Fibonacci sequence**. The diagram opposite shows the various subdivided wave patterns and the numbers of waves involved where:

Pattern	Number of waves	Total
x	5+3	8
y	3 + 5 + 5	13
z	5 + 3 + 5 + 3 + 5	21
w	y + z	34

However, market wave patterns do not always follow their 'theoretical' shape and **extensions** of an **impulse** wave can occur. It is very unusual to see an extension in the first wave – they are commonly seen in the third and fifth waves, especially in the third waves.

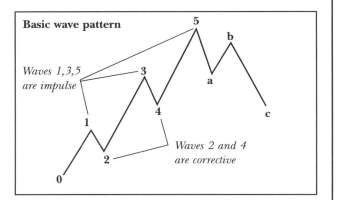

Basic wave pattern

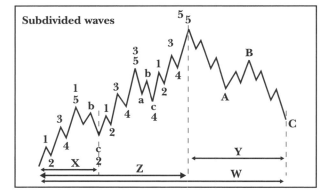

Subdivided waves

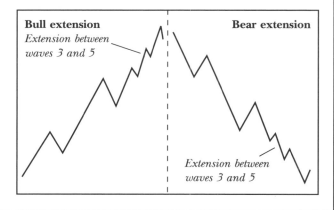

Bull extension — Bear extension

Elliott Wave Theory and Fibonacci Numbers

Patterns

Correction waves – a,b,c – can also exhibit patterns which are identified as follows:

- **Zig-zags** – 5,3,5

- **Flats** – 3,3,5

- **Triangles** – ascending, descending, contracting and expanding. In Elliott Wave Theory, triangles are always made up of 5 bars – a to e.

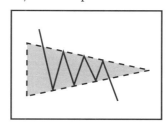

- **Complex** – Double, triple or multiple threes. In complex corrections these threes can be made up of combinations of zig-zags, flats and triangles.

These corrective patterns can become very complicated and difficult to recognise!

Ratio

Ratio analysis is used to determine where prices should move – a retracement is a movement in the opposite direction to the previous trend. Typically the Fibonacci ratios of 0.382, 0.618, 1.618 and 2.618 are used to predict price targets for retracements and combinations.

Time

It is not quite so easy to predict cycles based on time using Elliott Wave Theory. Although cycles exist it is more difficult to predict or identify significant peaks and troughs corresponding to Fibonacci numbers.

Bear zig-zag

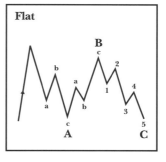
Flat

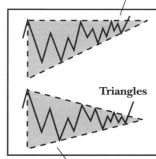
Ascending – Flat top, bottom sloping up

Triangles

Contracting or symmetrical – Top sloping down, bottom sloping up

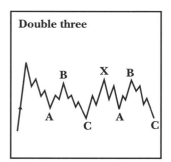
Double three

Waves, Numbers and Cycles

Elliott Wave Theory

Summary

- The underlying principle is that market prices are **cyclic** and can be identified according to **patterns**, **ratios** and **time**.

- A complete **cycle** is made up of **8 wave**s. In a bull market 5 waves up are followed by 3 down and vice versa in a bear market.

- Waves can be **expanded** into longer waves and **subdivided** in shorter waves. Thus a completed 5 bar wave can itself be seen as a single wave in what is known as a wave of **one higher degree**. Alternatively the third wave of a completed 5 wave structure can be sub-divided into 5 waves.

- **Impulse waves** may have **extensions**. Normally the third wave, less often the fifth and rarely the first wave.

- **Corrective waves** – a, b, c – are made up of **patterns** including:
  - Zig-zags
  - Flats
  - Triangles
  - Double, triple and multiple threes

- The **Fibonacci sequence** and **numbers** are an integral part of the theory – the numbers of waves, ratios of one wave to another, retracements of impulse waves and price targets for both impulse and corrective moves.

Elliott Wave Theory and Fibonacci Numbers

A bar chart of last trade daily FTSE -100 index values

Elliott Wave analysis is very complicated and different technical analysts may interpret the same chart in different ways. The various counts here are suggested Elliott wave patterns only – you may interpret the chart differently!

Waves, Numbers and Cycles

Gann Charts

W.D. Gann was a stock and commodity trader working in the first half of this century who reputedly made over $50 million in the markets. He made his fortune using methods which he developed for trading instruments based on relationships between price movement and time, known as time/price equivalents. There is no easy explanation for Gann's methods, but in essence he used angles in charts to determine support and resistance areas and predict the times of future trend changes. He also used lines in charts to predict support and resistance areas.

Gann noticed that the majority of price movements followed a simple ratio – typically they were 1/4, 1/2, 1 x, or 2 x the price at a particular starting point. This starting point was termed the **pivot point**. Sometimes the price movement was 1/3 or 2/3 the price from the pivot point. Gann also noticed that there was an important relationship between these price movements and time – in particular it was quite common to see a unit price movement take place in unit time. This Gann called **squaring the price** which lies at 45° from the pivot point providing the scales on both chart axes are the same.

Gann used a number of other lines to indicate future support and resistance areas for different price/time ratios using Gann Angles. These are expressed as **Time x Price**. For example, a 2 x 1 Gann Angle line is drawn such that for every two time units there is an increase in one price unit; a 1 x 2 line means that for every time unit increase the price increases twice.

Pivot Point
This is a particular point in a time and price chart when the trend direction changes. Depending on the instrument being charted, pivot points can be seen on a tick, hourly, daily, weekly etc. basis.

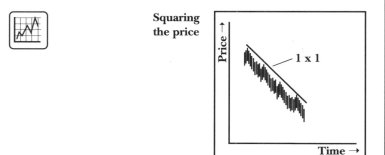

Squaring the price

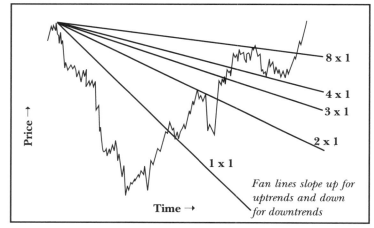

Fan lines slope up for uptrends and down for downtrends

Pivot points

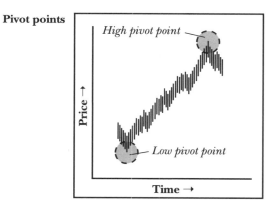

Gann Charts

Gann Lines

These are lines which can be drawn to predict the future levels of support and resistance calculated from a high and low pivot point.

All that is required is to divide the height of the price movement by the number of divisions required – typically 8 or 10. These lines then provide the forward support/resistance levels. Gann emphasised the importance of the 50% retracement level line.

Gann Angles

These are ascending/descending lines drawn from a high or low pivot point, each having a specific angle known as the Gann angle. The lines, projecting into the future, represent different rates of price movement/change with time.

The lines for Gann angles also provide an indication for support and resistance levels. As a price reaches and intersects a Gann angle you should see either support or resistance for this price.

Time x Price	Line angle	Time x Price	Line angle
1 x 8	82.50°	2 x 1	26.25°
1 x 4	75.00°	3 x 1	18.75°
1 x 3	71.25°	4 x 1	15.00°
1 x 2	63.75°	8 x 1	7.50°
1 x 1	45.00°		

Gann Charts

Gann lines, with their associated Gann angles, provide an enhanced indication of future support and resistance levels.

Gann lines

The price difference between the high and low pivot points has been divided into 10

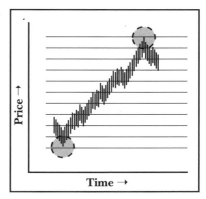

Gann angles

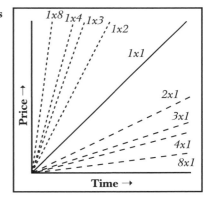

Gann Charts

A bar chart of weekly last trade DAX index values. The Time Price Equivalent is one price unit per interval for both Gann fans

A bar chart of weekly prices for Iomega Corporation shares. The Time Price Equivalent is one price unit per interval for the Gann fan

Gann Charts

GAS.L, Last Trade [Hi/Lo/Cl Bar] Weekly

25May92 – 18Jan97

GAS.L , Last Trade, Hi/Lo/Cl Bar,
08Dec96 221 210 217½

1 x 1
2 x 1
3 x 1
4 x 1
8 x 1

1 x 1
2 x 1
3 x 1
4 x 1
8 x 1

*A bar chart of weekly last trade British
Gas shares. The Time Price Equivalent is
⅝ units per interval for both Gann fans*

Sep92 Jan93 May Sep Jan94 May Sep Jan95 May Sep Jan96 May Sep Jan97

Pr
GBp
360
350
340
330
320
310
300
290
280
270
260
250
240
230
220
210
200
190
180
170

Charting Exercise

Although Gann Fans are available on the new version of Reuters Graphics, Elliott Wave software charting packages are only available for the specialist market. The following exercise allows you to try and find the Elliott Wave patterns in a chart.

Chart Exercise
Using the bar chart for weekly bid USD/DEM prices shown below indicate any Elliott Wave patterns you think are present. As this is quite a complicated task the start and finish points are indicated as I and V. Check your chart with that on page 132.

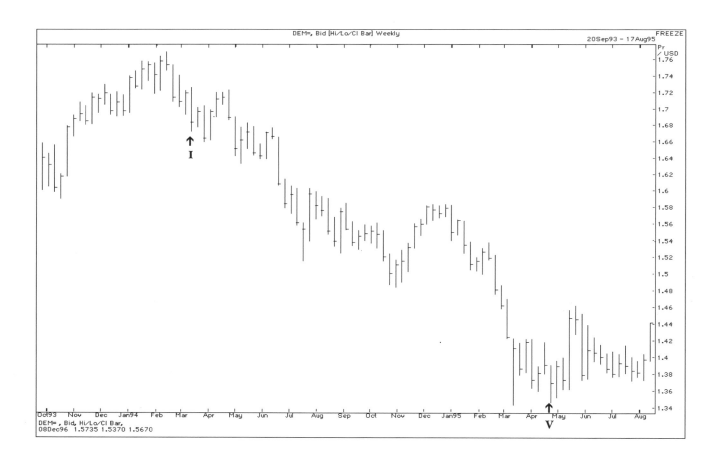

Summary

You have now finished the fifth section of the book and you should have a clear understanding of the following waves, numbers and cycles:

- Elliott Wave Theory

- Fibonacci Numbers

- Gann Charts

As a check on your understanding of this section you should try the Quick Quiz Questions. You may also find the Overview section to be a helpful learning tool.

Quick Quiz Questions

1. What are the four most important Fibonacci ratios and reciprocals of ratios? You should be able to quote the values to three decimal places.

2. In Elliott Wave Theory **corrective** waves – a, b, c – are made up of patterns. Name at least three of these patterns:

   i)

   ii)

   iii)

   iv)

3. Which of the following statements are true and which are false concerning Gann charts?

	True	False
a) The start position for Gann lines is termed the pilot point		
b) Gann Lines predict the future levels of support and resistance from a particular high or low start position		
c) A 1 x 8 Time/Price line means that for every 8 time units there is an increase of one price unit		
d) The 1 x 1 Time/Price line is known as squaring the price		

   You can check your answers on page 135.

Chart Exercise – Answer

Remember that Elliott Wave analysis is very complicated and different technical analysts may interpret the same chart in different ways. The various counts here are **suggested** Elliott wave patterns only – you may have interpreted the chart differently!

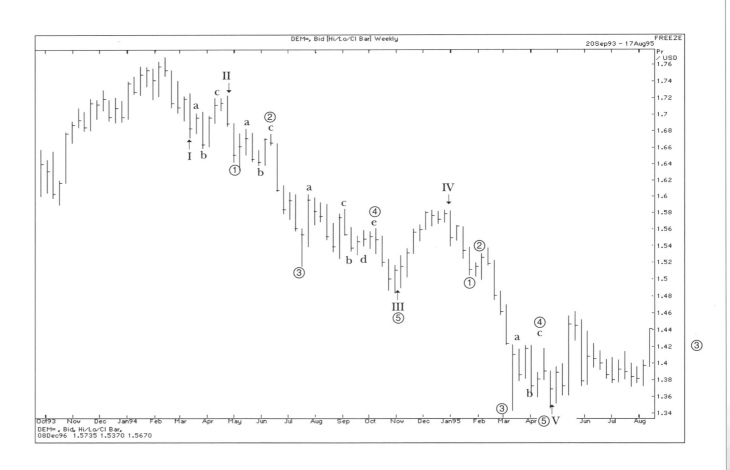

Overview

Fibonacci Numbers

- **Leonardo Pisano** or **Fibonacci** identified a mathematical sequence of numbers in the thirteenth century:

    0,1,1,2,3,5,8,13,21,34,55,89,144...

- Each number in the sequence is the **sum of the previous two digits**

- Ratio of any number to its **higher** number is **0.618**

- Ratio of any number to its **lower** number is **1.618**

- Ratio of **alternate numbers** is **2.618**

- Reciprocal value of **1.618** is **0.618**

- Reciprocal value of **2.618** is **0.382**

Waves, Numbers and Cycles

Elliott Wave Theory

- Elliott Wave Theory is applied to many markets and has three aspects – **Pattern, Time** and **Ratio**

- Devised by **Elliott** with the underlying principle that markets move in a **five wave pattern** in **the direction of the trend**, followed by a **three wave pattern in the counter direction**

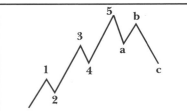

- Patterns of waves follow the **Fibonacci sequence of numbers**

- Fibonacci ratios of 0.382, 0.618, 1.618 and 2.618 are used to predict price targets for retracements and continuations

- Most common pattern shapes for correctional waves as opposed to impulse waves are:
    - **Zig-zags**
    - **Flats**
    - **Triangles**
    - **Complex – Double, triple and multiple threes**

Gann Charts

- **Gann's** methods for trading instruments were based on relationships between price movement and time, known a **time/price equivalents**

- **Gann Lines** are used in charts to predict future levels of Support/Resistance calculated from a high and low **pivot point**

- Support/Resistance lines for different time/price ratios are expressed as **Time x Price** lines. For example, 2 x 1 means one price unit increase for every 2 time units

- Ascending/descending lines drawn from a high or low pivot point, each have a specific angle known as the **Gann angle**

- Unit price movement in unit time is called **squaring the price**

Time x Price	Line angle	Time x Price	Line angle
1 x 8	82.50°	2 x 1	26.25°
1 x 4	75.00°	3 x 1	18.75°
1 x 3	71.25°	4 x 1	15.00°
1 x 2	63.75°	8 x 1	7.50°
1 x 1	45.00°		

Further Resources

Books

Elliott Wave Principle Applied to the Foreign Exchange Markets
Robert Balan, Financial Publications, 1989
ISBN   None

Elliott Wave Principle
Robert Prechter and Alfred Frost, Probus Publishing Co., 1990
ISBN   0 9327 5017 6

Mastering Elliott Wave
Glenn Neely, Probus Publishing Co., 1990
ISBN   0 9302 3344 1

Gann Made Easy: How to TradeUsing the Methods of W.D. Gann
W. McLaren

The W.D.Gann Method of Trading
Gerald Marisch
ISBN   0 9302 3342 5

Technical Analysis of Stocks and Commodities

Gann by C. Arnold
Vol. 1:3 (48-51), 1982/3

Gann Lines and Angles by R. Pardo
Vol. 3:5 (177-183), 1985

What K-wave? by J. Walker
Vol. 7:7 (227-229), 1989

Trading with Gann lines by D. Lamarr
Vol. 8:4 (142-144), 1990

The Elliott Wave: Sidebar
Vol. 12:3 (106-111), 1994

RFT Web Site at http://www.wiley-rft.reuters.com
This is the series' companion web site where additional quiz questions, updated screens and other information may be found.

Quick Quiz Answers

1. *What are the four most important Fibonacci ratios and reciprocals of ratios? You should be able to quote the values to three decimal places.*

0.382	0.618	1.618	2.618

2. *In Elliott Wave Theory corrective waves – a, b, c – are made up of patterns. Name at least three of these patterns:*

   i)   Zig-zags

   ii) Flats

   iii) Triangles

   iv) Double, triple and multiple threes

3. *Which of the following statements are true and which are false concerning Gann charts?*

	True	False
a) *The start position for Gann lines is termed the pilot point*		✔
b) *Gann Lines predict the future levels of support and resistance from a particular high or low start position*	✔	
c) *A 1 x 8 Time/Price line means that for every 8 time units there is an increase of one price unit*		✔
d) *The 1 x 1 Time/Price line is known as squaring the price*	✔	

Your notes

Your notes

This section of the book should take about 45 minutes of study time. You may not take as long as this or you may take a little longer – remember your learning is individual to you.

'You cannot get something good for nothing. You must pay with time, money or knowledge for success – W. D. Gann'

The Gann Method by John J. Blasic
Technical Analysis of Stocks and Commodities, Vol. 10:6 (268-271), 1992

'Asking the market what is happening is always a better approach than telling the market what to do'

Using Bollinger Bands by John Bollinger
Technical Analysis of Stocks and Commodities, Vol. 10:2 (47-51), 1992

Introduction

This final section in the book is concerned with the day-to-day activities of a few technical analysts. It has been included to give you a 'flavor' of what they do. But why are there technical analysts? The following brief summary of technical analysis may help to put the role of the practitioners and the techniques used in perspective.

The birth of technical analysis is widely agreed as occurring in Japan during the eighteenth century. This was the first time that prices were recorded with a view to predicting future events. Rice was the key commodity at that time, and the very first futures exchange came into being around 1700 to trade rice futures, or 'empty baskets' as they were known. A successful merchant and moneylender from the **Honma** family named **Munehisha**, together with his nephew **Mitsuoka**, are popularly recorded as having invented the Candlestick method of plotting price action. This method was little known outside of Japan until about 1989/90 when Steve Nison, an American analyst, succeeded in introducing and massively popularising the technique into Western markets.

Charles Dow, famed for the **Dow-Jones Index** and the **Dow Theory**, is the person who comes most readily to mind when talking of the modern history of charting and technical analysis. What is not so well known is that Charles Dow, founder of *The Wall Street Journal*, was also the originator of the Point and Figure method of charting. Dow's work up to his death in 1902 was principally concerned with stockmarkets.

WD Gann is another famous American whose work on commodities and stockmarkets spanned 50 years to 1950. A complete and unique branch of theory is named after him – Gann Theory. Between the years of 1940-1955, Ralph Nelson Elliott, another American formulated his theory – **Elliott Wave Theory** – again essentially a complete technical analysis branch in itself.

The beginning of the 1960s was a particularly difficult period for technical analysts as this was the time that the **Efficient Market Theory** held sway. This theory, held by fundamentalists in particular, suggested that price action in the market is random and cannot be predicted. It is also worth noting that up to this point all chart construction was accomplished by hand, both a time-intensive and laborious process. But all this was about to change particularly by events in the Foreign Exchange (FX) market.

Up to 1970 the FX market was a comparatively calm place compared with the frantic arena that it is today. Almost all trading took place between 9am and 5pm London time with participants reluctant to quote outside these hours. This was especially so in the US where prices were then quoted **inversely**, for example, USD/DEM. Indeed, in London, very often the first price quoted at around 9am would be virtually identical to that last quoted before 5pm the previous afternoon. Spot Yen was a minor currency for the dealing room junior to handle, along with the likes of the Singapore Dollar and the Saudi Riyal. But by late 1971 this situation was to change dramatically.

The reasons for the changes in 1971 have their origins in the Bretton Woods conference, held in 1944 in the US. This was when the framework for the post-World War II economic order was discussed. From this meeting came the World Bank (International Bank for Reconstruction and Development) and the International Monetary Fund (IMF). Crucially, all the mainline currencies were pegged to the US Dollar. As economic performances among nations diverged and with the reluctance of governments to revalue their currencies, it was clear that the Bretton Woods exchange parity agreement was in jeopardy. Temporary measures such as exchange controls and trade barriers failed and in the autumn of 1971 the US suspended the Gold Standard.

A Day in the Life of a Technical Analyst

The Bretton Woods exchange parity agreement was replaced with a new era of floating exchange rates.

The result of floating exchange rates was **volatility**, which was of an intensity that had not been seen before. This introduced profound new risk into the commercial world. Whereas previously companies had accepted exchange exposure with equanimity, they realised now that to hedge and lock in their exposure was a wise move. However, markets moving with no defined limits also offered the opportunity for speculative gain and the probability of loss for the foolish and unwary.

Thus arose the need to attempt to understand why prices moved in the way they did. Could prices be predicted? In 1974 the International Monetary Market (IMM) was established as a subsidiary of the Chicago Mercantile Exchange (CME). The IMM was set up to deal in financial futures and began with contracts for the mainline currencies against the dollar, plus an (unsuccessful) Certificate of Deposit contract. Chicago's fame grew from its expertise in trading commodity futures: it was the young traders from the commodity pits who moved across into the newly instituted IMM, bringing with them one of their principal tools – technical analysis.

To begin with, the IMM turnover was small and had little impact on the main FX market. However, as their market grew so did the confidence of the traders within it and before long their activities started to affect the massive Spot market. 'Who are these crazy people at the IMM?' was an increasingly common question to be heard in London in the mid-seventies. And what is this technique called technical analysis that they are all using?

1976 is a notable year in that it saw the introduction of the first commercial personal computer (PC) in the UK - the Commodore Pet. Seen as something of a novelty at the time it was not until IBM introduced its own machine in 1981, and set the standard for everyone else to follow, that the PC market took off. Computers can store vast quantities of data and then utilise this data in performing large numbers of complex mathematical calculations at astonishing speed. Here then was the final piece of the jigsaw that lit the blue touchpaper and sent the 'technical analysis rocket' into orbit.

The need to understand price action in the marketplace was ever greater due to increasing volatility. Somehow certain technical analysts seemed to have a very discernible edge over other market participants – they made consistently accurate calls. The techniques they used and their research into new techniques were ideally suited to the personal computer. It is probably true to say that if it was the wheel that revolutionised transport, then it was the PC that revolutionised technical analysis.

Today the power and speed of desktop PCs are constantly improving and what was considered to be a state-of-the-art machine a year ago is now out of date! Testing technical analysis ideas requiring massive computational power is now possible and was but a pipe-dream until recently. Right at the 'cutting edge' we have now a merging between traditional technical analysis and the new technologies of Neural Networks, Expert Systems, Fuzzy Logic etc. Astonishing advances have been made since the mid-1980s in analysing market behaviour, but might this only be the beginning?

To give you an idea of the real world of technical analysis, here are two brief diaries taken from the activities of analysts. Read on.

It's What People Say...

You know, I sometimes wonder why I do this job! Why didn't I go into accountancy after leaving school like my mother suggested – a regular nine-to-five job, good prospects, and little stress. Sorry!, I should have said – I'm a technical analyst working for a medium-sized bank advising the dealers on the technical perspective of the various markets that the bank's trading and investing in. This covers the spot FX desk, the guys trading Futures on LIFFE, CME, and CBOT, and – oh yes – we've got a big funds management division upstairs that I have to keep briefed on just about every equity market you can think of! You couldn't think of a less routine job – every day's different! It sure isn't 9-to-5, 7-to-7 might be more accurate when the markets are hectic. But in truth I love it! Let me tell you about a crazy day that's just passed.

News is the fuel that drives the markets. That's why dealers are always hanging on the latest headlines from news providers. Guess there's two types of news, the 'scheduled,' normally concerning prime economic data releases from the G7 countries... and then there's the 'bolt from the blue' variety. Fashions change, but for several years the key monthly economic indicators for the global markets have been the US employment figures issued at 1:30pm London time on the first Friday of each month. To be more specific it's the **Non-farm Payroll**[1] component, which 10 years ago no dealer had ever heard of! It's a strange world, time and again the two hours following the release of 'Non-farms' sees the most active and volatile trading in the whole month. The November figures were due on Friday the 6th of Dec, and I'd gone home on the Thursday night thinking of the virtually certain hectic day ahead plus prospects for my own trading position short of Dec FTSE futures on LIFFE. But more of that later.

There I was relaxing watching one of the kid's James Bond movies when the mobile rang. My treasurer on the line telling me that Greenspan had made comments in a late NY speech regarding 'inflated asset values' and 'euphoric markets'. Now if there's one guy on the planet that can send the world markets into a tail-spin with one sentence it's Alan Greenspan, the chairman of the mighty US Federal Reserve – effectively the US Central Bank. And here we had it, the dreaded 'bolt from the blue' news shock, and to cap it all, the night before the US employment figures! It was going to be a very early start in the morning – the boss had moved the morning strategy meeting to 7:30.

At my desk just after 6:00am and work like a mad thing preparing to brief the section heads at the 7:30 meeting. Far East[2] equity markets have taken a dive, it looks like gloom and doom for Europe on equities and interest rates. Suddenly I'm the most popular person in the bank, everybody, but everybody, wants to know what I think. *'Is this the start of the crash everyone's feared? Where are the downside targets? Isn't it overdone, shouldn't it bounce from here? etc etc'.* At least my own position short of FTSE is looking good, and for that I offer up thanks to Alan Greenspan – last month I was cursing him!

It would take forever to cover all the markets we looked at in that meeting, so I'll just pick one – US T-Bond futures on Chicago's CBOT – and then show you what I got up to in my own trading.

I've been into Candlesticks since reading Steve Nison's book and I like combining them with trendlines, slow stochastics, and Bollinger bands – a volatility envelope analysis. Every analyst has his own 'pet' analyses and the ways he/she interprets them. Successful technical analysis is about using a cocktail of different techniques that complement each other rather than using one single analysis in isolation – and I'm no different.

---

1   Non Farm Payroll: that portion of the US employment figure reported monthly that includes all reported (ie, through government offices and corporate reporting) unemployment, and excludes informal or farm-related help.
2   Far East: refers to trading in the Asian markets.

This is the daily candlestick chart of the December T-Bond on the CBOT.

❶ Bit of backtracking (OK, boasting really). I'd thought that the sideways structure that formed during October was shaping up like a triangle –breakout should resume the uptrend. So fingers crossed and gave the bond desk a buy signal should 111 20/32 be broken on the strong uptrending market developing during the 29th – **Candle A**. All rather excited when it went like a rocket and closed at 112 19/32 – virtually a big figure in – but getting 'right-side' of the market is just half of the story, once you're in you have to decide when to get out!

❷ OK the Close on the 29th was outside the Bollinger volatility envelope, but the key thing was the envelope was expanding – top line going up, bottom going down – volatility therefore rising. It was a big breakout of a major horizontal resistance at 111 28/32 so we thought this might be one to ride. Next few days saw some topsy-turvy conditions but no doubts the bulls had control. Come late evening on the 12th Nov got called at home by our late shift. T-Bonds about to close outside the Bollingers with the top and bottom Bollinger lines 'in synch' (both moving together) – **Candle B**. Now one of the golden rules of the game is *'Bulls make money, Bears make money, but greedy Pigs just make losses!'* So prudence rules, put some money in the till, and we close half of the long position at 114 28/32. Two days later and we've got pretty well the same situation but this time we've run slap bang into what we see as the outer channel line. So close out the remaining 25 long position at 115 9/32 just before the close, thank you very much indeed and good night nurse!

4USZ6, Last Trade [Candle][Bol. Bands 9 1.618], Last Trade [Slow Stoch. 9,3,3] Daily
10Jun96 – 14Dec96   FREEZE

Major resistance at 111²⁸/₃₂

Old gap

Stochastic divergence 1

Stochastic divergence 2

❸ However, in the trading world you can't rest on your laurels for long, question *'What do we do next?'* The guys on the Bond desk were split as to what strategic position to run, if any. The older heads were saying *'the trend is your friend'* so let's get back long, the younger *'burn 'em up'* brigade that it had gone too far and was 'bound' to reverse soon – DANGEROUS!

Me? – I preferred sitting on the fence!

❹ Close of Friday 22nd Nov saw a classic Stochastic Divergence (**Stoch Diverge 1**). The T-Bond desk were mumbling that I'd lost my nerve (don't they ever have any of their own trading ideas?) and so I told them *'Sell the Opening'* on the 25th. What looked good at the off, 115 5/32, had a nasty smell about it near the close, 115 15/32, so swallowed hard and told the late shift to cut it. Just 10 pips loss but I sure was popular with the bond jockeys next morning - short memories, what about the 3 big figures I'd recently made them!

❺ 4th December and I'm getting interested in the bonds again. As a down day develops it's possible we could be left with another confirmed stochastic divergence (**Stoch Diverge 2**) plus a nice long black candle would give us a pattern with characteristics of an Evening Star – a potent bull market reversal signal. So it's agree what we'll do with the bond desk if we get the right set-up near the close, make the call to the brokers and sell at 115 22/32 on the death – **Candle C**. Next day we get an acceleration on the downside – **Candle D** – and I'm the blue-eyed boy again! However, tomorrow's the dreaded Non-farm payrolls so the boss says he wants the profit on half the position come what may – and we leave a 'profit take' at the expected resistance level of 114 18/32 which happily gets executed. Shortly afterwards 'Bang!' and Mr Greenspan pulls the trigger!

❻ Next morning as I said all markets are in turmoil and we haven't even heard the 'Non-farms' yet! Boss must be thinking of his bonus as he says he wants the profit and to be flat before the figures. So everybody looks at me and says where? – Thanks! Well we know it's going to open loads lower and will be trading for 10 minutes before the figures. There's an old gap formed between the 4th and 5th November, 113 3/32 to 113 10/32. Old gaps act as support/resistance and the market adage is to look to see this halfway between the gap. So fingers and legs crossed we put in an order on the off to buy at 113 7/32 and 'bingo' we get filled! A few minutes later out come the 'Non-farms' significantly better than expected and it's all change for a bull rally! How lucky can you be! Boss was walking round like a Cheshire cat!

But what about my own trading in this mayhem – I do like to try and keep my hand in with a bit of 'live action' besides advising people all day long. My normal patch for trading is the S&P 500 futures contract on the CME and the FTSE future on LIFFE – main reason for trading these contracts is to stay on the ball for Equity markets given that I get so many *'What's going to happen?'* calls from the fund boys upstairs. Of late I'd been flying the Union Jack and just concentrating on the FTSE.

As said I was short of the Dec. FTSE futures going home on Thursday night. For short term trading I like half hourly charts, and round about midday on the 5th we'd developed a nice set-up.

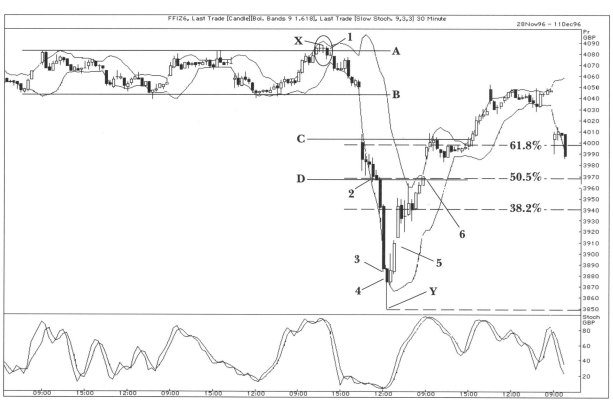

❶ The ringed area that shows a long white candle followed by two Dojis (a Doji is a small candle where the Open and Close are about the same – looks like a cross and is a sign of weakness in a trending market). The next candle was a long black that enveloped the bodies of the previous three candles. As it was also a confirmed stochastic divergence I sold just before the close of the half hour at 4078. It all developed very nicely on the downside going into the daily close, so I decided to hold the position overnight. My hope was we might challenge the **B** line of the **A/B** channel that had dictated trading for the previous two days.

❷ Well overnight Uncle Greenspan came and did me a big favour and we opened gap down, not only under **B** but also beneath the 'one channel down' line at **C**. I have this theory about parallel channels, that when they break the market moves one and then two channels down as the energy released is dissipated. So I was looking

for a rendezvous with the second channel down at **D** which we duly got just before 10:30. Nearly took the whole position out as I could hardly think given all the phone calls I was getting plus all the shouting and shrieking going on around the room! However, I cashed in for half the position at 3967 and decided to give the rest a bit more rope.

❸ Good (lucky?) decision as the bears came in as we approached midday and gave the market a right seeing to! Just before 12:00 I'd got one of my classic scenarios – a truly wicked long black candle **3** closing outside the volatility envelope with upper and lower bands moving 'in synch'. Sit on the fence time, don't be greedy! So out we come to go flat at 3888 – not bad result for what's not even a day's trading!

❹ Always a dangerous time after a big profit. It's so easy to let euphoria and 'I'm the greatest' swamp rational analysis, and before you know what's happened you've done something really stupid and handed a large part of the profits back! So having learnt this painful message in the past several times, I keep telling myself to calm down and concentrate. Next candle **4** looks very much like a Hammer – a classic bear market reversal pattern. However, with the Non-farms only an hour away I haven't got the guts – maybe I'm being sensible for once. Normally I'd go like a shot to get long at the end of the period marked by candle **5** – but Non-farms were but seconds away. Out they come and with screams of *'Buy, buy...'* echoing around the room I manage to get some on board and go long at 3926.

❺ Well not a lot of chance to do much more as throughout the afternoon it seemed 'the whole world' wanted to speak to me. But for my running position the eternal problem – where to come out? Haven't said, but I'm also a bit of a Fibonacci fan – that centuries old Italian was one clever bloke! I particularly like the fibonacci retracements for pullbacks from big moves – 38.2%, 50%, 61.8%. The overall move spawned by the Greenspan shambles was **X** to **Y** as marked on the chart together with the 'fib' retracement levels based off this **X – Y** move. You know sometimes one just has days where everything goes right, and this was one of them! 50% was 3968 and just before 5:30pm we manage to nick in and close out during the APT (late electronic trading as opposed to pit open outcry) session.

What a day, you don't get too many like that thank goodness! Feeling shattered as I've been at the desk for 12 hours without a break. You can tell that it's been a great day for the dealing room from all the excited buzz, and I think there's a bit of a party mood afoot. Yep, the Boss says all down the local wine bar and the champagne's on him!

An Early Start ...

Pete is a technical analyst working for ABC who specialise in providing live technical analysis on the various markets over Reuters. Two of Pete's main clients are Danny and Hans.

Danny is a speculator running a small fund. He trades in various markets, usually holding positions for no longer than a few days.

Hans is a corporate dealer at XYZ Bank in Frankfurt. His client is an importer of Italian shoes who requires a favourable exchange rate to purchase foreign currency.

Pete advises both Danny and Hans on timing the market.

It's 6.45 am in London, on 9th October. Pete is at his desk. He checks the overnight movements on the currency and US T-Bond markets to get an indication of how the European markets will open.

Between 7.00 – 8.00 am – when most LIFFE Markets open – Pete analyses the markets he will be covering today. He writes a technical commentary on the markets providing trading recommendations for the day ahead.

He reads the *Reuter Insight Debt News Analysis*, **BXNB**, on his RT to see if any important economic data is due today. The US Gross Domestic Product (GDP) figure is out at 1.30pm – Pete envisages an active afternoon!

The next few hours are quiet which allows Pete time to prepare his Elliott Wave outlook of the US Stock Market for a client in New York...

```
---- REUTER INSIGHT CONSENSUS OF GLOBAL MARKET FORECAST      BXNB
GMT ----------KEY INDICATORS----------FORECAST---RANGE---PREVS
0630   THU    JPN. INDUSTRIAL PROD OCT  +3.4  PCT +2.5/+4.1  +1.5
0630   THU    JPN. INDUST PREL Y/Y OCT  +6.0  PCT +5.1/+6.7  +3.4
0745   THU    FRA. GDP (PREL)   Q/Q Q3  +0.8  PCT +0.3/+1.1  -0.4
0745   THU    FRA. GDP (PREL)   Y/Y Q3  +1.1  PCT +0.9/+1.4  +0.5
1330   THU    CAN. AVG. WEEKLY ERN SEP  +2.6  PCT +2.6/+2.7  +2.6
0030   FRI    JPN. CONSUMER PRICES OCT  -0.1  PCT -0.1/+0.1  +0.4
0030   FRI    JPN. CPI (NAT'L) Y/Y OCT  +0.2  PCT +0.1/+0.3  FLAT
0030   FRI    JPN. CONSUMER PRICES NOV  FLAT  PCT -0.3/+0.2  FLAT
0030   FRI    JPN. CPI TOKYO  Y/Y  NOV  +0.1  PCT -0.1/+0.4  -0.1
N/A    FRI    JPN. JOB RATIO       OCT  0.72  PCT 0.71/0.73  0.71
28-NOV-0748. MON360 L2856487
                                             MORE
```

It's 11.30 – Pete's phone rings.

Pete: Hello.

Danny: Hi, it's Danny. What do you think of DEM/ITL?

Pete: I'll take a look and call you back in 5.

Pete calls up a **weekly bar chart** of DEM/ITL using Reuter Technical Analysis. This allows Pete to get an overall picture of the medium-term trend. Pete examines over 3 years of price action and has the following observations:

1. A major bull market ended at 1275.00 in March 1995. The market has been a bear since. The **impulsive** moves are down whereas the **corrective** moves are up.

2. The 15 and 30 week **moving averages** are bearishly aligned, with recent rally attempts thwarted by these.

3. Important **supports** are at 945.00 and 897.00. **Resistances** are at 1036.70. 1099.50 and 1171.00.

Impulsive moves are the sharp moves which go to make up the overall trend. **Corrective** moves are temporary reactions against the trend as profit-taking ensues.

The short-term average is under the long-term average. Both are pointing down.

Having ascertained the medium-term trend, Pete now calls up a **daily bar chart** of DEM/ITL using Reuter Technical Analysis. Pete examines daily – sometimes intra-day – charts to time entry into the medium-term trend. Pete observes the following:

1. The market failed to hold under 3rd October low of 989.40, rebounding back above 990.00 level.

2. 9-day **RSI** basing in oversold territory having shown a bull divergence.

Pete's **conclusions**:
The medium-term bear trend looks over extended in the short-term. A correction of between **38.2** and **61.8**% of the impulsive decline from 1036.70 looks due over the next few weeks.

Once the correction is complete, the medium-term bear trend should resume towards support at 945.00 and 897.00 as the next impulsive phase gets underway.

Breach of the 61.8% retracement at 1018.00 will warn that the bear trend is in the process of reversing.

Once Pete has decided what DEM/ITL will do over the next few weeks he rings Danny...

Signs of waning bear momentum are noted when the market cannot sustain a push into new lows.

Another sign of fading bear momentum.

Corrective moves usually retrace 38.2 to 61.8% of the preceding impulsive move. These retracement values are based on Fibonacci numbers.

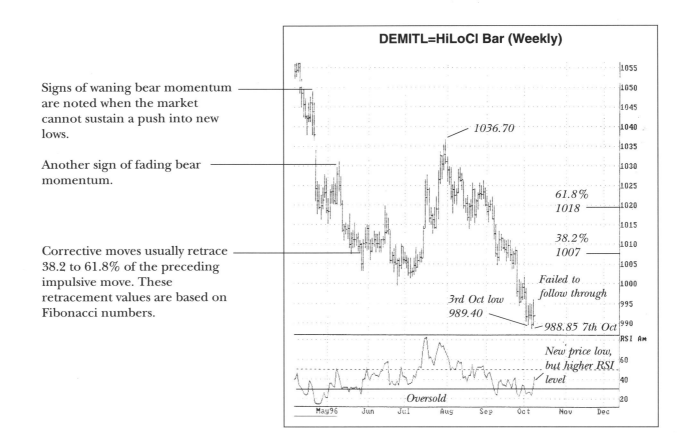

DEMITL=HiLoCl Bar (Weekly)

1036.70

61.8%
1018

38.2%
1007

Failed to follow through

3rd Oct low
989.40

988.85 7th Oct

New price low, but higher RSI level

Oversold

Pete: Hi, Danny. DEM/ITL looks good for a rally to 1007/1012 over the next few weeks. Play the long side with a stop-loss under 988.85.

Danny: Thanks Pete – I'll call my broker.

} *A stop-loss level is a pre-defined point at which a losing trade is exited. Stops are used to minimise market risk.*

Pete pops out for lunch and on his return about 1.20 pm starts to monitor US T-Bond futures ahead of the US GDP data. The figure is out at 1.30 pm and is weaker than expectations. The Bond markets rise initially but swiftly reverse early gains. Five minutes later Pete's phone rings again...

Danny: Pete, have you seen the BTPs?

} *Buoni del Tesoro Poliennali (BTP) are Italian fixed rate Treasury bonds with varying maturities from 5, 10 and 30 years – the most liquid market being for 10 year bonds.*

Pete: Yeah, I hope you're short!

Danny: Looks like I should be – with T-Bonds struggling and DEM/ITL going to 1007 - 12!

The Bond markets sell off and the DEM rallies throughout the afternoon. About 3.30 pm Hans phones Pete...

Hans: Pete I want to buy some Lire. When should I get in?

Pete: I'd wait a week or two. The market's due for a correction towards 1007/1012 before the next leg down to 945/897. Give me a call then and we'll discuss short-term timing.

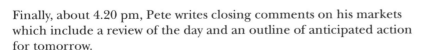

Finally, about 4.20 pm, Pete writes closing comments on his markets which include a review of the day and an outline of anticipated action for tomorrow.

Summary

You have now finished the final section of the book and you should have some understanding and knowledge of the following:

- The development of technical analysis

- The basic tools and techniques used by technical analysts covering –

  - Chart types
  - Patterns
  - Indicators
  - Waves, numbers and cycles

- The ways in which technical analysts use the various tools and techniques

If you want to study more about the ways traders and analysts use technical analysis, go to the **Further Resources** section.

Further Resources

Books

Market Wizards: Interviews with Top Traders
J. Schwager, Harper Business, 1989
ISBN   0 8873 0601 1

Intermarket Technical Analysis
John Murphy, J. Wiley & Sons, 1991
ISBN   0 4715 2433 6

The Psychology of Technical Analysis
Tony Plummer, Probus Publishing Co., 1993
ISBN   1 55738 543 2

Steidlmayer on Markets
J. Peter Steidlmayer, J. Wiley & Sons, 1989
ISBN   0 4716 2115 3

Mind Over Markets
J.F. Dalton, E.T. Jones and R.B. Dalton, Probus Publishing Co., 1993
ISBN   1 55738 489 4

Trading for a Living
Dr. Alexander Elder, J. Wiley & Sons, 1993
ISBN   0 471 59224 2

The Futures Game
Richard J. Teweles and Frank J. Jones, McGraw-Hill Book Company,
Second Edition
ISBN   0 07 063734 2

The Elements of Successful Trading
Robert P. Rotella, New York Institute of Finance, 1992
ISBN   0 13 20579 6

Schwager on Futures - Technical Analysis
Jack D. Schwager, J. Wiley & Sons, 1996
ISBN   0 471 02051 6

Technical Analysis of Stocks and Commodities

The publishers of this monthly journal can be contacted at the following address:

> Technical Analysis Inc.
> 4757 California Avenue, SW
> Seattle
> WA 98116
> USA

Reprints of the articles mentioned in the *Further Resources* sections of this book can be obtained from Technical Analysis Inc. together with a CD-ROM of all the monthly journals, 1982 – 1994.

RFT Web Site at http://www.wiley-rft.reuters.com
This is the series' companion web site where additional quiz questions, updated screens and other information may be found.

Your notes

Glossary of Technical Analysis Terms
courtesy of Charles J. Kaplan, President of Equity Analytics, Ltd.

This is a slightly edited version of the Equity Analytics technical analysis glossary. The full version can be found on the internet at the URL address, *http://www.e-analytics.com/glossary/glossar1.htm*. The Publisher will not be responsible for any inaccuracies found in the glossary below. Queries should be addressed to Equity Analytics, Ltd. at *glossaries@equityanalytics.com*.

A

Accumulation
The first phase of a bull market. While most investors are discouraged with the market, and earnings are at their worst, some investors start buying shares. Or, and addition to a traders position.

Adaptive Filter
Continuously updating the weighting of past prices for smoothing or forecasting purposes.

Advance/Decline Line
Each day's declining issues are subtracted from that day's advancing issues. The difference is added to (subtracted from if negative) a running sum. Failure of this line to confirm a new high is a sign of weakness. Failure of this line to confirm a new low is a sign of strength.

Alpha
The premium an investment earns above a set standard. This is usually measured in terms of the DOW Industrials or the S&P 500. How the stock performs independent of the market.

Arbitrage
The simultaneous buying and selling of two or more different, but closely related securities, in different markets to take advantage of price disparities.

Area Pattern
When a stock or commodities upward or downward trend has stalled. The sideways movement in price which follows forms a pattern. Some of these patterns may have predictive value. Examples of these patterns are head & shoulders, triangles, pennants, flags, wedges, and broadening formations.

Arms Index
This is an indicator which relies on advances and declines in the stock market. A reading above 1 or in some software 100, is bearish. A number below 1 or in some software 100, is bullish. The higher the number the more bearish. The lower the number, the more bullish. In the normal course of trading, this number is usually between about 40 and 60. Very high or very low numbers occur infrequently. The formula is: ((# of advancing issues/ # of declining issues)/ (Total up volume/ Total down volume)).

Ascending Trend Channel
The tops of an ascending price line develop along a line parallel to the trend line which slopes upward across the bottoms of the down waves.

At-The-Money
An option whose strike price is equal to the price of the underlying security.

B

Back Testing
Optimizing a trading strategy on historical data and applying it to fresh data to see how well the strategy works.

Technical Analysis Glossary

Bear Trap
A false signal which indicates that the rising trend of a stock or index has reversed when in fact it has not.

Bear Market
A longer period of time when prices in the market are generally declining.

Bear Spread
An option strategy with maximum profit when the price of the underlying security declines. Maximum loss occurs if the underlying security rises in price. The strategy involves the purchase and simultaneous sale of options. Puts or calls can be used. A higher strike price is purchased and a lower strike price is sold. The options have the same expiration date.

Beta
The degree of sensitivity of a stock in relation to swings in the market.

Beta (Coefficient)
The degree of risk which cannot be decreased by diversification. A stock with a beta greater than 1 will rise faster or decline faster than the overall market. A stock with a beta lower than 1 will rise slower or decline slower than the overall market.

Black Scholes Option Pricing Model
A model used to estimate the price of an option.

Box Spread
Option arbitrage in which a profitable position is established with no risk. One spread is established with call options. The other spread is established using put options.

Breadth (Market)
Relates to the number of issues participating in a market move. The move can be either up or down. As a rally develops, and the number of advancing issues is declining, the rally is suspect. As a decline develops, and the number of declining issues falls, the decline becomes suspect.

Bullish
Generally a longer period of time in which prices rise.

Bull Spread
An option strategy in which the maximum profit is attained if the underlying security rises in price. Either calls or puts can be used. The lower strike price is purchased and the higher strike price is sold. The options have the same expiration date.

Bull Trap
A false signal which is generated which indicates that the price of a stock or index has reversed to an upward trend but which proves to be false.

Butterfly Spread
An option strategy combining a bull and bear spread. Three strike prices are used. The lower two strike prices are used in the bull spread and the higher two strike prices are used in the bear spread. Either puts or calls can be used. This strategy has limited risk and limited profit.

C

Calendar Spread
An option strategy where a trader sells a shorter term option and buys a longer term option. Both options have the same strike price. For instance, a March 50 call might be sold and a May 50 call purchased.

REUTERS

Calendar Combination
An option strategy where a trader opens a call calendar spread and a put calendar spread at the same time. The strike price of the calls is higher than the strike price of the puts.

Call Option
A contract which gives the purchaser the right not the obligation to purchase the underlying security at a specific price within a specific time frame.

Call Price
The price at which a bond or preferred stock can be called in by the issuing authority.

Candlestick Charts
A charting method originally developed in Japan. The high and low are described as shadows and plotted as a single line. The price range between the open and close is plotted as a rectangle on the single line. If the close is above the open, the body of the rectangle is white. If the close of the day is below the open, the body of the rectangle is black.

Capitalization Weighted Index
A stock index which is computed by adding the capitalization's of each individual stock and dividing by a predetermined divisor. The stocks with the greatest market values have the greatest impact on the index.

Chaikin Oscillator
An oscillator created by subtracting a 10 day exponential moving average from a 3 day exponential moving average of the accumulation distribution line.

Contingent Order
An order given to a trading desk to buy stock and sell a covered call option. It is given as one order.

Conversion Arbitrage
The simultaneous purchase of a stock, the purchase of a put, and the sale of a call. It is a riskless transaction.

Channel
Used in charting, it allows the user to draw parallel lines connecting the low points and the high points. It can be ascending or descending.

Convertible Security
One security which is convertible into another. It is generally used with convertible preferred stock and convertible bonds. There is a specific rate at which the security can be converted.

Cover
The act of buying back in a closing transaction an option which was originally written.

Covered
Writing an option when the writer also own the underlying security on a one to one ratio. A short call is covered if the underlying security is owned. A short put is covered if the underlying security is also short in the account. A short call is covered if a long call of the same underlying security is owned in the same account with the same or lower strike. A short put is covered if a long put of the same underlying security is owned in the same account with a strike price equal to or greater than the strike of the short put.

Confirmation
At least two indicators or indexes corroborate a market turn or trend. In the case of the stock market, with respect to Dow Theory, it would be the Dow Industrials and the Dow Transports.

Congestion Area
At a minimum, a series of trading days in which there is no or little progress in price.

Correction
A price reaction of generally ⅓ to ⅔ of the precious gain.

Cup And Handle
A pattern on bar charts. The pattern can be as short as seven weeks and as long as 65 weeks. The cup is in the shape of a U. And the handle has a slight downward drift. The right hand side of the pattern has low trading volume.

D

Daily Range
The difference between the high and low during one trading day.

Delta
The amount an option will change in price for a one point move in the underlying security.

Delta Neutral
An options strategy designed so that the position is insensitive to movements in the underlying security. It can be composed of options/options or options/underlying security. It is a careful calculation of offsetting long and short positions.

Diagonal Spread
An options strategy in which the purchased options have a longer maturity than the written options. The purchased options also have different strike prices. Examples of Diagonal Spreads are: diagonal bull spreads, diagonal bear spreads, and diagonal butterfly spreads.

Discount
An option is trading at a discount if it is selling for less than its intrinsic value. If a future is trading for less than the price of the underlying security, it is considered to be trading at a discount.

Double Bottom/ Double Top
These are reversal patterns. It is a decline or advance twice to the same level (plus or minus 3%). It indicates support or resistance at that level.

Drawdown
Reduction in account equity from a trade or series of trade.

E

Early Exercise
Early Exercise Prior to expiration, the exercise or assignment of an option.

Elliot Wave Theory
Originally published by Ralph Nelson Elliot in 1939. It is a pattern recognition theory. It holds that the stock market follows a pattern of five waves up and three waves down to form a complete cycle. Many technicians believe that this pattern can hold true for as short a time period as one day. However, it is generally used to measure long periods of time in the market.

Ex-Dividend
The day when the dividend is subtracted from the price of a stock. The ex-dividend date is the date on which this takes place. Investors who own the stock are paid their dividend on that date. Investors who are short the stock must pay the dividend on that date.

Exercise
The right granted under the terms of a listed options contract. Call holders exercise their right to buy the underlying security. Put holders exercise their right to sell the underlying security. There is generally an exercise limit placed by the options exchange. This is to prevent a group of investors or an individual investor from cornering the market on an underlying security.

Equivolume Chart
Richard Arms created this type of chart. It measures the relationship between price and volume. Price is measured on the vertical axis and volume is measured on the horizontal axis.

Exponential Moving Average
An exponential moving average is a form of a weighted moving average. Eg: To construct a 20 day exponential moving average you must first construct a 20 day simple moving average. This simple moving average is the starting point for the exponential moving average. Assume that the simple moving average value for day 20 is 42; the simple moving average value for day 21 is 43; and the simple moving average value for day 21 is 44. We then subtract the day 20 moving average value from day 21 simple moving average value and get a difference of 1.00. This value (1.00) is multiplied by an exponent. In this case, the exponent is .1. We then add .1 to the simple moving average value of day 20. The exponential moving average value of day 20 now becomes 42.100. And this goes on indefinitely. To calculate the exponent, divide 2 by the time period. In our case, we divided 2 by 20 to arrive at .1.

F

Fair Value
Describes the worth of an options or futures contract. On a daily basis, fair value is published pertaining to the S&P futures. When fair value falls below a predetermined value, traders sell the cash index and buy futures. When fair value rises above a predetermined value, traders buy the cash index and sell futures.

Fibonacci Ratio
The relationship between two numbers in the fibonacci sequence. The sequence for the first three numbers is 0.618, 1.0, and 1.618. In general terms the fibonacci series is 1, 1, 2, 3, 5, 8, 13, 21, 34, 55, 89, etc.

First Notice Day
The first day a buyer of a futures contract can be called upon to take delivery.

Float
The number of shares outstanding for a particular common stock.

Floor Broker
A trader on the floor of an exchange who executes orders for people without access to the trading area.

Fundamental Analysis
Analysis of a security which takes into consideration sales, earnings, assets, etc.

Fuzzy Systems
Systems which process inexact information inexactly. It describes ambiguity instead of uncertainty of an occurrence.

G

Gamma
It measures the amount the delta changes for a 1 point move in the underlying security.

Good Till Canceled
An order placed with a broker meaning that it is good until either filled or canceled. In practice, this order has to be re-confirmed twice annually.

H

Head & Shoulders Pattern
This can also be inverted. It is a reversal pattern And it is one of the more common and reliable patterns. It is comprised of a rally which ends a fairly extensive advance. It is followed by a reaction on less volume. This is the left shoulder. The head is comprised of a rally up on high volume exceeding the price of the previous rally. And the head is comprised of a reaction down to the previous bottom on light volume. The right shoulder is comprised of a rally up which fails to exceed the height of the head. It is then followed by a reaction down. this last reaction down should break a horizontal line drawn along the bottoms of the previous lows from the left shoulder and head. This is the point in which the major decline begins. The major difference between a head and shoulder top and bottom is that the bottom should have a large burst of activity on the breakout.

Horizontal Spread
An options strategy where the options have the same strike and different expiration dates.

I

Implied Volatility
A measurement of the volatility of a stock. Current price rather than historical price is used. Generally, if the price of an option rises without a corresponding rise in the underlying equity, implied volatility is considered to have risen.

Index Option
An option whose underlying security is an index. An example would be the S&P 100 (OEX). A trader can buy index options and bet on the direction of the OEX.

Intermarket Spread
A spread using futures contracts in one market spread against futures contracts in another market. An example would be the Yen spread against the Deutschemark.

In-The-Money
A call option with a strike price below the underlying equity. A put option with a strike price above the underlying equity.

Inside Day
A day in which the total range of price is within the range of the previous day's price range.

Island Reversal
A trading range where there is an exhaustion gap down, then prices trade in a narrow range, then there is a breakaway gap up. This leaves a sort of island of prices in the middle. If the trading range is only one day, it is considered a one day reversal.

J, K

L

Leaps Long
Term Equity Anticipation Securities. Currently, these are long term options with expirations up to 2½ years.

Limit Order
An order to buy or sell at a fixed price. A person can also place a limit order with discretion. This enable the broker to buy or sell within a small range, usually ⅛ or ¼ of a point.

Limit Up/ Limit Down
Commodity exchange restriction on the maximum amount of movement up or down that a commodity can trade in a given day.

Local
A futures trader in the pit of a commodity exchange who buys or sells for his own account.

Lognormal Distribution
A statistical distribution often applied to stock prices. It implies that stock prices can rise infinitely but can not fall below zero.

M

Margin
The minimum amount of money required to buy or sell a security. The investor is using borrowed money.

Margin Call
The demand by a broker to an investor to put up money because his security(s) have declined in value. There are minimum amounts of capital required by the exchanges or the broker.

Market Maker
An exchange member who makes a market by buying and selling for his own account when the public is not buying and selling.

Market Order
An order to buy or sell a security at the present market price. As long as there is a market for this security, the order will be filled. This type of order takes precedence over all other orders.

Market Not Held Order
This is a market order. However, the investor is giving the floor trader the discretion to execute the order when he feels it is best. If the floor trade feels that the market will decline, he may hold the order to try to get a better fill. This order may not get filled.

Market If Touched
An order with the floor broker which becomes a market order if a trigger price is reached.

Momentum
The strength behind an upward or downward movement in price. Graphically, momentum is represented as a horizontal line which fluctuates above and below an equilibrium line.

Moving Average
Moving averages are one of the oldest technical indicators in existence. A basic definition of a moving average is that it is the average price of a security at a specific point in time. A moving average shows a trend. The purpose of the moving average is to show the trend in a smoothed fashion.

Moving Average Convergence/Divergence (MACD)
The crossing of two exponentially smoothed moving averages. They oscillate above and below an equilibrium line.

N

Noise
Fluctuations in the market which can confuse one's interpretation of market direction.

Negative Divergence
When two or more indicators, indexes, or averages, fail to show confirming trends.

O

Odd Lot
A block of stock consisting of less than 100 shares. When odd lots trade, a premium is usually tacked on by the specialist or market maker. These receive the least favorable price and trade last.

Open Interest
The net total amount of outstanding contracts in a future or option.

Options Clearing Corporation (OCC)
The issuer of all listed options on all exchanges.

Out Of The Money
A call whose strike price is above the current market price of the underlying equity. A put whose strike price is below the current price of the underlying security.

Overbought
Market prices that have risen too steeply and too quickly.

Oversold
Market prices that have declined too steeply and too quickly.

P

Point And Figure Chart
A chart which plots price only. Xs are placed in boxes representing up days; and Os are placed in boxes representing down days. There is no provision for time in point and figure charting. As long as the trend remains the same, the Xs or Os are placed above or below each other. When a reversal takes place, the next vertical column starts the next trend.

Portfolio Insurance
In order to protect a portfolio of stocks an investor may sell index futures or buy index put options for downside protection.

Position Limit
The maximum number of option contracts on the same side of the market which can be held by any one investor or group of related investors. A long call and a short put are on the same side of the market. A long put and a short call are on the same side of the market.

Premium
The price an investor pays the writer of an option above the options intrinsic value.

Price Earnings Ratio
The ratio of the price of a stock to the earnings per share. Or total annual profit divided by the number of shares outstanding.

Program Trading
Trades based on signals from computer programs. These are usually entered directly from the traders computer to the market's computer system. Program trading accounts for an increasingly larger and larger portion of all trades throughout the day. Additionally, these large trades may be hedged by an offsetting position in index futures.

Public Book
The public orders to buy or sell a security which are not market orders.

Put Option
A contract which gives the purchaser the right, not the obligation, to sell a security at a specific price in for a specified period of time.

Put Call Ratio
The ratio of put trading volume divided by the call trading volume. Moving averages can be used to smooth this chart out.

Q

R

Ratio Calendar Combination
An options strategy where a trader has at the same time a ratio calendar spread using calls and a ratio calendar spread using puts. The strike price of the calls is greater than the strike price of the puts.

Ratio Calendar Spread
Option strategy using either puts or calls, whereby one sells more near term options than longer term options are purchased. All options have the same strike price.

Ratio Spread
Option strategy using either puts or calls. The trader purchases a certain amount of options and then sells a larger amount of out of the money options.

Ratio Write
Buying stock and selling calls against the stock. It can also be constructed by shorting stock and then selling puts against the short stock.

Relative Strength
A comparison of an individual stock's performance to that of a market index. Most times the S&P 500 or the Dow Jones Industrial Index are used for comparison purposes. It is calculated by dividing the stock price by the index price. A rising line indicates that the stock is doing better than the market. A declining line indicates that the stock is not doing as well as the market.

Resistance
A price level where a security's price stops rising and moves sideways or downward. It indicates an abundance of supply. Because of this, the stock may have difficulty rising above this level. There are short term and longer term resistance levels.

Return On Assets
Net earnings of a company divided by its assets.

Return On Equity
Net earnings of a company divided by its equity.

S

Secondary Market
A market available to trade securities after their initial public offering. The New York Stock Exchange is an example of a secondary market.

Selling Short
Selling a security and then borrowing the security with the intent of replacing that security at a lower price than it was borrowed. The short trader is betting that the price of the security will go down.

Specialist
An exchange member who keeps the public book, maintains an orderly and efficient market, buys and sells for his own account.

Short Interest
Shares that have been sold short and not yet repurchased.

Short Interest Ratio
A ratio which tells how many days it would take to buy back all the share which have been sold short. A short interest ratio of 2 would indicate that it would take 2 trading days to buy back all the shares which have been sold short. This is based on the current volume.

Slippage
The difference between estimated and actual transaction costs. The difference is usually comprised of commissions and price differences.

Spread Strategy
An option strategy having both long and short options on the same underlying security.

Spot Month
The current trading month. Also known as the front month in commodity trading.

Spot Price
The current cash price for which a commodity is trading at a specific time and place.

Stop Order
An order placed which is not at the current market price. It becomes a market order once the security touches the specified price. Buy stop orders are placed above the present market price. Sell stop orders are placed below the present market price.

Stop Limit Order
This is similar to a stop order. It is an order which becomes a limit order once the specified price is touched.

Stop And Reverse
A stop that when hit is a signal to close the current position and open an opposite position. A trader holding a long position would sell that position and then go short on the same security.

Straddle
An options strategy where the purchase or sale of an equal number of puts and calls is made. The same strike price and expiration date is the same for all.

Strangle
An options strategy which is a combination involving a put and a call with different strike prices with the same expiration.

Support
A price level at which declining prices stop falling and move sideways or upward. It is a price level where there is sufficient demand to stop the price from falling.

Synthetic Stock
Using options, it is equivalent to the stock. A long call and a short put is a synthetic long stock. A long put and a short call is a synthetic short stock.

T

Theta
A measurement of how much an option's price decays for every one day that passes.

Trending Market
Price moves in a single direction and it usually closes on an extreme for the day.

Trendline
Constructed by connecting a series of descending peaks or ascending troughs. The more times a trendline has been touched increases the significance of a break in the trendline. It can act as either support or resistance.

U

Uncovered Option
This is sometimes referred to as a naked option. It is when a trader writes an option without owning the underlying security. It is a position with large risk.

V

Variable Ratio Write
An options strategy in which a trader writes 2 or more options contracts for every 100 shares owned. Each option has a different strike price.

Vega
A measurement of how much an options price changes for a 1% change in volatility.

Vertical Spread
An options strategy which is also a spread where the options have different strike prices but the same expiration dates.

Volatility
The measurement of how much an underlying security fluctuates over a period of time.

W

Warrant
A long term security which is similar to an option. A stock warrant usually allows a trader to purchase one share of stock at a fixed price for a certain period of time.

Write
To write an option is to sell an option. The person who sells the option is considered to be the writer.

X, Y, Z

Your notes

Listing of Stock Exchanges Around the World

courtesy of Haksu Kim of Pacific Investment Research, Inc.

The full version can be found on the internet at the URL address, *http://www.fawpir.com/exchange.htm*. The Publisher will not be responsible for any inaccuracies found in the listing below. Kindly address any queries to Pacific Investment Research, Inc. via their home page at *http://www.fawpir.com*.

North America

Canada

Alberta Stock Exchange
Stock Exchange Tower
21st Floor
300 Fifth Avenue Southwest
Calgary, Alberta T2P 3C4, Canada
Phone: 403-974-7400
Fax: 403-237-0450
Web site: http://www.alberta.net

Montreal Exchange
Tour de la Bourse
P.O. Box 61
800 Victoria Square
Montreal, Quebec H4Z 1A9, Canada
Phone: 514-871-2424
Fax: 514-871-3553
Web site: http://www.me.org

Toronto Stock Exchange
The Exchange Tower
2 First Canadian Place
Toronto, Ontario M5X 1J2, Canada
Phone: 416-947-4520
Fax: 416-947-4547
Web site: http://www.tse.com

Vancouver Stock Exchange
Stock Exchange Tower
P.O. Box 10333
609 Granville Street
Vancouver, British Columbia V7Y 1H1, Canada
Phone: 604-689-3334
Fax: 604-688-6051
Web site: http://www.vse.ca

Winnipeg Stock Exchange
2901-One Lonbard Avenue
Winnipeg, Manitoba R3B 0B3, Canada
Phone: 204-942-8431

United States

Securities and Exchange Commission
Division of Corporate Finance
450 5th Street, NW
Washington, District of Columbia 20549, U.S.A.
Phone: 202-272-2800

New York Stock Exchange
Eleven Wall Street
New York, New York 10005, U.S.A.
Phone: 212-656-3000
Fax: 212-656-2126
Web site: http://www.nyse.com

American Stock Exchange
86 Trinity Place
New York, New York 10006-1881, U.S.A.
Phone: 212-306-1000
Fax: 212-306-8376
Web site: http://www.amex.com

Nasdaq Stock Market
Business Development
1735 K Street, NW
Washingto, District of Columbia 20006-1500, U.S.A.
Phone: 202-728-8840
Fax: 202-496-2699
Web site: http://www.nasdaq.com

Arizona Stock Exchange
2800 N. Central Avenue
Suite 1230
Phoenix, Arizona 85004, U.S.A.
Phone: 602-222-5858
Web site: http://www.azx.com

Boston Stock Exchange
One Boston Place
Boston, Massachusettes 02108, U.S.A.
Phone: 617-723-9500
Fax: 617-523-6603
Web site: http://www.bostonstock.com

Chicago Stock Exchange
440 S. Lasalle Street
Chicago, Illinois 60605, U.S.A.
Phone: 312-663-2980
Fax: 312-663-2396
Web site: http://www.chicagostockex.com

Chicago Board of Options Exchange
400 S. LaSalle Street
Chicago, Illinois 60605, U.S.A.
Phone: 312-786-5600
Web site: http://www.cobe.com

Chicago Mercantile Exchange
30 South Walter Drive
Chicago, Illinois 60606, U.S.A.
Phone: 312-930-3457
Web site: http://www.cme.com

Cincinnati Stock Exchange
49 E. Fourth Street, Suite 205
Cincinnati, Ohio 45202, U.S.A.
Phone: 312-786-8803

New York Mercantile Exchange
4 World Trade Center
New York, New York 10048, U.S.A.
Phone: 212-938-2222
Web site: http://www.nymex.com/

Pacific Stock Exchange
301 Pine Street
San Francisco, California 94104, U.S.A.
Phone: 415-393-4000
Fax: 415-393-4018
Web site: http://www.pacificex.com/

Philadelphia Stock Exchange
1900 Market Street
Philadelphia, Pennsylvania 19103, U.S.A.
Phone: 215-496-5102
Fax: 215-496-5653
Web site: http://www.phlx.com

Latin America

Argentina

Buenos Aires Stock Exchange
Sarmiento 299, 2nd Floor
Buenos Aires 1353, Argentina
Phone: 54-1-317-8980
Fax: 54-1-317-2676
Web site: http://www.bcba.sba.com.ar/

Rosario Board of Trade
Cordoba 1402
Rosario
Santa Fe 2000, Argentina
Phone: 54-41-21-3471
Fax: 54-41-24-1019

Barbados

Stock Exchange of Barbados
5th Fl., Central Bank of Barbados
Church Village
St. Michael, Barbados
Phone: 809-436-9871
Fax: 809-429-8942

Bermuda

Bermuda Stock Exchange
5th Floor, Washington Mall
Church Street
Hamilton HM FX, Bermuda
Phone: 441-292-7212
Fax: 441-292-7619
Web site: http://www.bsx.com

Bolivia

Bolivian Stock Exchange
av. 16 de Julio XL 1525
Edif Mutual La Paz-Piso3, PO Box 12521
La Paz, Bolivia
Phone: 591-2-39-2911/14

Brazil

Rio de Janeiro Stock Exchange
Praca XV de Novembro, 20
Centro
Rio de Janeiro 20010-010, Brazil
Phone: 55-21-271-1001
Fax: 55-21-221-2151
Web site: http://www.bvrj.com.br/

Sao Paulo Stock Exchange
(BOVESPA)
Rua XV de Novembro, 275
Sao Paulo 01013-001, Brazil
Phone: 55-11-233-2000
Fax: 55-11-233-2099
Web site: http://www.bovespa.com.br/indicei.htm

Chile

Santiago Stock Exchange
(Bolsa de Comercio de Santiago)
Calle La Bolsa 64
Santiago, Chile
Phone: 56-2-698-2001
Fax: 56-2-672-8046
Web site: http://www.bolsantiago.cl/ingles

Chile Electronic Exchange
Huerfanos 770, 14th Floor
Santiago, Chile
Phone: 56-2-639-4699
Fax: 56-2-639-9015
Web site: http://www.bolchile.cl/presenta

Colombia

Bogota Stock Exchange
(Bolsa de Bogota)
Carrera 8, No. 13-82
Piso 7, 8, y 9
Santafe de Bogota, Colombia
Phone: 57-1-243-6501x100
Fax: 57-1-243-3170
Web site: http://www.bolsabogota.com.co/

Medellin Stock Exchange
Carrera 50, No. 50-48, Piso 2
PO Box 3535
Medllin, Colombia
Phone: 57-4-260-3000
Fax: 57-4-251-1981

Occidente Stock Exchange
Calle 10 #4-40, Apartado Aereo 11718
Piso 13 Edificio Bolsa de Occidente, Cali
Valle del Cauca, Colombia
Phone: 57-23-889-8400
Fax: 57-23-889-9435
Web site: http://cali.cetcol.net.co/~bolsaocc

Costa Rica

Bolsa Nacional de Valores, S.A.
Edificio Cartagena, 4th Floor
Calle Central Ave., Primera
San Jose, Costa Rica
Phone: 506-222-8011
Fax: 506-255-0131
Web site: http://merica.cool.co.cr/usr/bolsa/bolsa.html

Dominican Republic

Santo Domingo Securities Exchange
Edificio Disesa
Ave. Abraham Lincoln, Suite 302
Santo Domingo, Dominican Republic
Phone: 809-567-6694
Fax: 809-567-6697

Ecuador

Gyayaquil Stock Exchange
Baquerizo Moreno 1112
Guayaquill, Ecuador
Phone: 593-4-30-7310
Fax: 593-4-56-1871

Stock Exchange of Quito
Ave. Amazonas 540 y Carrion Bvo. Piso
Apartado 17-01-3772
Quito 3772, Ecuador
Phone: 593-2-52-6805
Fax: 593-2-50-0942

El Salvador

El Salvador Stock Exchange
Edificio La Centroamericana, 6 piso
Alameda Roosevelt #3107
San Salvador, El Salvador
Phone: 503-298-4244
Fax: 503-232-898

Guatemala

National Stock Exchange of Guatemala
4a Calle 6-55, Zona 9
Guatemala City, Guatemala
Phone: 502-2-34-2479
Fax: 502-2-31-4509

Honduras

Honduras Stock Exchange
2 Calle - 3 Ave
Edificio Martinez Valenzuela, 1 piso
San Pedro Sula, Cortes, Honduras
Phone: 504-53-4410
Fax: 504-53-4480

Bolsa Centroamerica de Valores
Edificio Sonisa
Costado este Plaza Bancatlán
Tegucigalpa, Honduras
Phone: 504-39-1930 / 1931
Fax: 504-32-2700
Web site: http://www.bcv.hn/

Jamaica

Jamaica Stock Exchange
3rd Fl., Bank of Jamaica Building
Nethersole Place, PO Box 1084
Kingston, Jameica
Phone: 809-967-3271/4
Fax: 809-922-6966

Mexico

Mexico Stock Exchange
(Bolsa Mexicana de Valores SA de CV)
Paseo de la Reforma 255
Mexico DF 06500, Mexico
Phone: 52-5-726-6600
Fax: 52-5-726-6793
Web site: http://www.bmv.com.mx/bmvenglish/

Nicaragua

National Stock Exchange of Nicaragua
(Bolsa de Valores de Nicaragua S.A.)
Edificio Oscar Perez Cassar
Km 41/2 Carretera a Masaya
Managua, Nicaragua
Phone:505-278-3830
Web site: http://www.bolsanic.com/

Panama

Panama Stock Exchange
Calle Elvira Mendez y Calle 52
Edificio Vallarino, Plant
Panama
Phone: 507-269-1966
Fax: 507-269-2457

Paraguay

Asuncion Stock Exchange
Estrella 540
Asuncion, Paraguay
Phone: 595-21-450-103
Fax: 595-21-442-445

Peru

Lima Stock Exchange
Pasaje Acuna 191
Lima, Peru
Phone: 51-14-267-939
Fax: 51-14-267-650
Web site: http://www.bvl.com.pe/english/

Trinidad and Tobago

Trinidad and Tobago Stock Exchange
65 Independence Square, Port of Spain
Trinidad, West Indies
Phone: 868-625-5107/9
Fax: 868-623-0089
Web site: http://stockex.co.tt/

Uruguay

Montevideo Stock Exchange
(Bolsa de Valores de Montevideo)
Miisiones 1400
Montevideo 11000, Uruguay
Phone: 598-2-916-5051
Fax: 598-2-916-1900
Web site: http://www.bvm.com.uy/i1.htm

Bolsa Electronica de Valores del Uruguay S.A.
Misiones 1537 Piso 6
CP 11.000 Montevideo, Uruguay
Phone.: 598-2-97.00.00
Fax.: 598-2-97.00.01
Web site: http://bevsa.comintur.com.uy/

Venezuela

Caracas Stock Exchange
(Bolsa de Valores de Caracas)
Calle Sorocaima Entre Av. Tamanco Y
Venezuela, EDF, Atrium, Piso 1, El Rosal
Caracas 1060-A, Venezuela
Phone: 58-2-905-5511
Fax: 58-2-952-2640

Western Europe

Austria

Vienna Stock Exchange
(Wiener Börsekammer)
Wipplingerstrasse 34
A-1011 Vienna, Austria
Phone: 43-1-534 99 400
Fax: 43-1-534 99 444
Web site: http://www.vienna-stock-exchange.at/boerse/

Belgium

Antwerp Stock Exchange
(Effectenbeursvennootschap van Antwerpen c.v.)
Korte Klarenstraat, 1
2000 Antwerpen, Belgium
Phone: 32-3-233-8016
Fax: 32-3-232-5737

Brussels Stock Exchange
(Brouse de Bruxelles)
Palais de la Bourse
Rue Henri Maus, 2
1000 Bruxelles, Belgium
Phone: 32-2-509 12 10
Fax: 32-2-511 95 00

Cyprus

Cyprus Stock Exchange
Chamber Building
38, Grivas Ohigenia Ave. & 3 Oeligiorgis Street
P.O. Box 1455
Nicosia, Cyprus
Phone: 357-2-44 95 00
Fax: 357-2-45 86 30
Web site: http://www.cse.com.cy/

Denmark

Copenhagen Stock Exchange
(Kobenhavns Fondsbors)
6, Nikolaj Plads
P.O. Box 1040
DK-1007 Copenhagen K, Denmark
Phone: 45-33-93 33 66
Fax 45-33-12 96 13

Finland

Helsinki Stock Exchange
(Helsingin Arvopaperiporssi)
P.O. Box 361
00131 Helsinki, Finland
Phone: 358-0-173 30 1
Fax: 358-0-173 30 999
Web site: http://www.hse.fi/english_index.html

France

Paris Stock Exchange
(La Bourse de Paris)
39 Rue Cambon
75001 Paris, France
Phone: 33-1-4927 1000
Fax: 33-1-4927-1171
Web site: http://www.bourse-de-paris.fr

Germany

German Stock Exchange
(Deutsche Börse AG)
Börsen Strasse 14
60284 Frankfurt am Main 1, Germany
Phone: 49-69-210 10
Fax: 49-69-299 77 514
Web site: http://www.exchange.de/fwb/fwb.html

Greece

Athens Stock Exchange
10 Sophocleous Street
Athens 105 59, Greece
Phone: 30-1-32 10 424
Fax: 30-1-32 13 938
Web site: http://www.ase.gr/

Ireland

Irish Stock Exchange
28 Anglessea Street
Dublin 2, Ireland
Phone: 353-1-677 88 08
Fax: 353-1-677 81 13

Italy

Italian Stock Exchange Counsil
(Consiglio Di Borsa)
Piazza degli Affari, 6
20133 Milan, Italy
Phone: 39-2-724 26 336
Fax: 39-2-720 24 333
Web site: http://www.borsaitalia.it/

Luxembourg

Luxembourg Stock Exchange
(Societe de la Bourse de Luxembourg SA)
11 Avenue de la Porte-Neuve
BP 165
L-2227 Luxembourg
Phone: 352-47 79 36 1
Fax: 352-47 32 98

The Netherlands

Amsterdam Stock Exchange
(Amsterdam Effectenbeurs)
Beursplein 5
P.O. Box 19163
1000 GD Amsterdam, The Netherlands
Phone: 31-20-523 45 67
Fax: 31-20-523 49 50

Norway

Oslo Stock Exchange
(Oslo Bors)
P.O. Box 460-Sentrum
0105 Olso I, Norway
Phone: 47-22-34 17 00
Fax: 47-22-42 68 47
Web site: http://www.nettvik.no/finansen/oslobors/engelsk/

Portugal

Lisbon Stock Exchange
(Borsa de Valores de Lisboa)
Edificio da Bolsa
Rua Soeiro Pereira Gomes
1600 Lisboa, Portugal
Phone: 351-1-790 9904
Fax: 351-1-795 2021

Oporto Stock Exchange
(Bolsa de Valores do Oporto)
Palacio de Bolsa
Rua Ferreira Borges
4000 Oporto, Portugal
Phone: 351-2-200 2476
Fax: 351-2-200 2847

Spain

Barcelona Stock Exchange
(Bolsa de Barcelona, Databolsa S.A.)
Passeig de Gracia 19
08007 Barcelona, Spain
Phone: 34-3-401-3541
Fax: 37-3-401-3859
Web site: http://www.borsabcn.es/

Madrid Stock Exchange
(Bolsa de Madrid)
Plaza de la Lealtad 1
28014 Madrid, Spain
Phone: 34-1-589 2600
Fax: 34-1-589 1417
Web site: http://www.bolsamadrid.es/homei.htm

Sweden

Stockholm Stock Exchange
(Stockholm Fondbors)
Kallargrand 2
P.O. Box 1256
S-111 82 Stockholm, Sweden
Phone: 46-8-613 8800
Fax: 46-8-411 6849

Switzerland

Swiss Exchange

Selnaustrasse 32
Postfach
CH-8021 Zürich,
Switzerland
Phone: 41-1-229 21 11
Fax: 41-1-229 22 33
Web site: http://www.bourse.ch/

Turkey

Istanbul Stock Exchange
(Istanbul Menkul Kiymetler Borsas)
Rihtim Cad. No. 245
Erenhan, Tophane, Karakoy
Istanbul 80031, Turkey
Phone: 90-212-252 4800
Fax: 90-212-298 2500
Web site: http://www.ise.org/

United Kingdom

London Stock Exchange
London EC2N 1HP, United Kingdom
Phone: 44-171-797-1000
Fax: 44-171-410-6807
Web site: http://www.stockex.co.uk/aim/index.htm

International Stock Exchange
Throgmorton Street
London EC2N 1HP, United Kingdom
Phone: 44-171-588 2355
Fax: 44-171-410 6807

Eastern Europe

Armenia

Yerevan Stock Exchange
22 Sarian Street
Center
Yerevan, Armenia
Phone: 374-252-5801
Fax: 374-215-1548

Bulgaria

Bulgarian Stock Exchange
1 Macedonia Square
12th Floor, Room 5
1000 Sofia, Bulgaria
Phone: 359-2-81-5540
Fax: 359-2-87-5566

Croatia

Zagreb Stock Exchange
Ksaver 208
10000 Zagreb, Croatia
Phone: 385-1-142-8455
Fax: 385-1-142-0293
Web site: http://www.zse.hr/

Czech Republic

Prague Stock Exchange
Rybna 14
110 00 Praha, Czech Republic
Phone: 42-2-2183-2191
Fax: 42-2-2183-3031

Estonia

Tallinn Stock Exchange
Ravala 6
10143 Tallinn, Estonia
Phone: 372-6-408-840
Fax: 372-6-408-801
Web site: http://www.tse.ee/main_e.htm

Hungary

Budapest Stock Exchange
Deak F.U. 5
1052 Budapest, Hungary
Phone: 36-1-117-5226
Fax: 36-1-118-1737
Web site: http://www.fornax.hu/fmon/index.html

Latvia

Riga Stock Exchange
Aldis Duntares
Doma Laukums 6
LV 1885 Riga, Latvia
Phone: 371-7-212-431
Fax: 371-7-820-504
Web site: http://www.rfb.lv/

Lithuania

National Stock Exchange of Lithuania
Ukmerges 41
2600 Vilnius, Lithuania
Phone: 370-2-723-871
Fax: 370-2-724-894
Web site: http://www.nse.lt/

Macedonia

Macedonian Stock Exchange
Mito Hadzivasilev No.20
91000 Skopje, Republic of Macedonia
Phone: 389-91-122 055
Fax: 389-91-122 069
Web site: http://www.mse.org.mk/

Republic of Moldoa

Moldoa Stock Exchange
Stefan cel Mare blvd. 73, Room 302
Chisinau, MD2001, Republic of Moldova
Phone: 3732-222-266
Fax: 3732-228-969, 226-351
Web site: http://www.moldse.com/

Poland

Warsaw Stock Exchange
Nowy Swiat 6/12
00-400 Warsaw, Poland
Phone: 48-22-628-3232
Fax: 48-22-628-1754
Web site: http://yogi.ippt.gov.pl/gielda/

Romania

Bucharest Stock Exchange
(Bursa de Valori Bucuresti - BVB)
Doamnei Str. 8
Bucuresti 70421, Romania
Phone: 40-1-323-0900
Fax: 40-1-323-5732
Web site: http://www.delos.ro/bse/

Russia

Moscow Central Stock Exchange
Ilyinka Street, 3/8
Building 3,4
103012 Moscow, Russia
Phone: 7-095-921-2551
Fax: 7-095-297-1-9391

Russian Stock Exchange
40 Herzen Street
Moscow, Russia
Phone: 7-095-230-2698

Russian Trading System
Chayanova 15, bld5
Moscow 125267, Russia
Phone: 7-095-705-9031/9032
Fax: 7-095-733-9515
Web site: http://www.rtsnet.ru/engl/default.stm

Siberian Stock Exchange
Frunze, 5
PO Box 233
63104 Novosibirsk, Russia
Phone: 7-3832-21-0690

St. Petersburg Stock Exchange
274 Ligovsky Pr.
198084 St. Petersburg, Russia
Phone: 7-812-298-8931
Fax: 7-812-296-1080

International Stock Exchange of Vladivostock
10-a Aleutskaya Street
690091 Vladivostock, Russia
Phone: 7-4232-228-009
Fax: 7-4232-226-798

Serbia

Belgrade Stock Exchange
Vladimira Popovica No. 6, BO2
11070 Belgrade, Serbia
Phone: 381-11-22-4049
Fax: 381-11-222-4355

Slovak Republic

Bratislava Stock Exchange
Vysoka 17
PO Box 151
814-99 Bratislava, Slovak Republic
Phone: 42-7-386-102
Fax: 42-7-386-103

RM-System Slovakia, a.s.(Slovakia OTC Markets)
Zamocke schody 2/A
P.O. BOX 301
810 00 Bratislava, Slovak Republic
Phone: 421-7-5329211, 412
Fax: 421-7-5329218, 414
Web site: http://www.rms.sk/indexe.htm

Slovenia

Ljubljana Stock Exchange
(Ljubljanska Borza vrednostnih papirjev d.d.)
Slovenska c. 56
61000 Ljubljana, Slovenia
Phone: 386-61-171-0211
Fax: 386-61-171-0213
Web site: http://www.ljse.si/

Asia/Pacific

Australia

Australian Stock Exchange
Exchange Centre
20 Bond Street
Sydney, NSW 2000, Australia
Phone: 61-2-227-0000
Fax: 61-2-227-0885
Web site: http://www.asx.com.au/

Bangladesh

Dhaka Stock Exchange
Stock Exchange Building
9F Motijheel Commercial Area
Dhaka 100, Bangladesh
Phone: 880-2-956-4601
Fax: 880-2-956-4727

China (People's Republic of China)

Shanghai Securities Exchange
15 Huangpu Road
Shanghai 200080, People's Republic of China
Phone: 86-21-306-8888
Fax: 86-21-306-8505

Shenzhen Stock Exchange
15/F International Trust & Investment Building
Hong Ling Zhong Road
Shenzhen, People's Republic of China
Phone: 86-755-558-3929
Fax: 86-755-559-4074

Hong Kong

Stock Exchange of Hong Kong
1/F, One & Two Exchange Square
Central, Hong Kong
Phone: 852-522-1122
Fax: 852-810-4475
Web site: http://www.sehk.com.hk/

Hong Kong Futures Exchange
Suite 605-608 Asia Pacific Finance Tower
Citibank Plaza
3 Garden Road
Central, Hong Kong
Phone: 852-2842-9333
Fax: 852-2845-2043
Web site: http://www.hkfe.com/

India

Ahmedabad Stock Exchange Association Ltd.
Manek Chowk
Ahmedabad 380 001, India

Bangalore Stock Exchange
Uni Building, Miller Tank
Vasanthanagar
Bangalore 560 052, India
Phone: 91-812-22-0163

Bhubaneshwar Stock Exchange Association
217 Budhraja Building
Jharpara Cuttak Road
Bhubaneshwar 751 006, India

Calcutta Stock Exchange
7 Lyins Range
Calcutta 700 001, India
Phone: 91-33-20-6957
Fax: 91-33-20-2514

Cochin Stock Exchange Ltd.
Exchange House
38/1431 Kaloor Road Extension
Ernakulum, Kochi-682035,, India

Coimbatore Stock Exchange
Chamber Towers
8/732 Avinashi Road
Coimbatore 641 018, India

Delhi Stock Exchange Association
3 & 4/4B Asaf Ali Road
West Plaza, I.G. Stadium
New Delhi 110 002, India
Phone: 91-11-335-2951
Fax: 91-11-332-6182

Guwahati Stock Exchange Ltd.
Saraf Building Annexe
A.T. Road
Guwahati 781 001, India

Hyberabad Stock Exchange Ltd.
Bank Street
Hyderabad 500 001, India

Jaipur Stock Exchange Ltd
Rajasthan Chamber Bhawan
M.I. Road
Jaipur 302 003, India

Kanara Stock Exchange Ltd
4th Floor, Rambhavan Complex
Kodialbail
Mangalore 575 003, India

Ludhiana Stock Exchange Association Ltd
Lajpat Rai Market, Clock Tower
Ludhiana 141 008, India

Madras Stock Exchange
11 Second Line Beach
Exchange Building
Madras 600 004, India
Phone: 91-44-512-237
Fax: 91-44-514-897

Madhya Pradesh Stock Exchange Ltd.
67, Bada Sarafa
Indore 452 002, India

Mangalore Stock Exchange Limited
4th Floor, Rambhavan Complex
Kodiabail
Mangalore 575 003, India

Meerut Stock Exchange Ltd.
Kingsway Building
345 Bombay Bazar
Meerut Cantonment 250 001, India

Mumbai Stock Exchange
Phiroze Jeejeebhoy Towers
Dalal Street
Mumbai 400 001, India
Phone: 91-22-265-5860
Fax: 91-22-265-8121
Web site: http://www.bseindia.com/

National Stock Exchange of India
Mahendra Towers, "A" Wing
1st Floor, RBC, Worli
Bombay 400 018, India
Phone: 91-22-493-2555
Fax: 91-22-493-5631
Web site: http://www.nseindia.com/

OTC Exchange of India
92/93 Market Tower "F"
Cuffe Parade
Bombay 400 005, India
Phone: 91-22-218-8164
Fax: 91-22-218-8511

Pune Stock Exchange Ltd.
1177, Budhwar Peth
Bank of Maharashtra Building, 2nd Floor
Bajirao Road
Pune 411 002, India

Saurashtra Kutch Stock Exchange Ltd.
4, Swaminarayan Gurukul Building
Dhebarbhai Road
Rajkot 380 002, India

Uttar Pradesh Stock Exchange Association Ltd.
Padam Towers
14/113 Civil Lines
Kanpur 208 001, India

Vadodara Stock Exchange Ltd.
101 Paradise Complex
Tilak Road, Sayaji Gunj
Vadodara 390 005, India

Indonesia

Jakarta Stock Exchange
Jl. Jenderal Sudirman Kav. 52-53
Jakarta 12190, Indonesia
Phone: 62-21-515-0515
Fax: 62-21-515-0220
Web site: http://www.jsx.co.id/

Surabaya Stock Exchange
Gedung Medan Pemuda 5th Floor
Jl. Pemuda No. 27-31
Surabaya 60271, Indonesia
Phone: 62-31-51-0646
Fax: 62-31-51-0823
Web site: http://www.bes.co.id/

Japan

Tokyo Stock Exchange
2-1, Nihonbasi-Kabuto-cho
Chuo-ku, Tokyo 103, Japan
Phone: 81-3-3666-0141
Fax: 81-3-3663-0625
Web site: http://www.tse.or.jp/

Osaka Stock Exchange
8-16, Kitahama 1-chome
Chuo-ku, Osaka 541, Japan
Phone: 81-3-229-8643
Fax: 81-6-231-2639
Web site: http://www.ose.or.jp/index_e.htm

Nagoya Stock Exchange
3-17, Sakae 3-chome
Naka-ku, Nagoya 460, Japan
Phone: 81-52-262-3171
Fax: 81-52-241-1527
Web site: http://www.iinet.or.jp/nse-jp/index-e.htm

Japan Securities Dealers Association
Tokyo Shoken Building
5-8, Kayabacho 1-chome
Nihonbashi, Chuo-ku, Tokyo 103
Phone: 81-3-3249-5501
Fax: 81-3-3249-3020

Korea

Korea Stock Exchange
33, Yoido-dodng
Youngdeungpo-ku
Seoul 150-010, Korea
Phone: 82-2-780-2271
Fax: 82-2-786-0263
Web site: http://www.kse.or.kr/

Malaysia

Kuala Lumpur Stock Exchange
4th Floor, Exchange Square
Off Jalan Semantan, Damansara Heights
50490 Kuala Lumpur, Malaysia
Phone: 60-3-254-6433
Fax: 60-3-256-1261
Web site: http://www.klse.com.my/

Nepal

Nepal Stock Exchange
PO Box 1550
Saarc Region on
Kathumandu, Nepal
Phone: 977-1-41-5210
Fax: 977-1-41-6461

New Zealand

New Zealand Stock Exchange
8th Floor, Caltex Tower
286-292 Lanton Quay
Wellington, New Zealand
Phone: 64-4-472-7599
Fax: 64-4-473-1470
Web site: http://www.nzse.co.nz/

Pakistan

Karachi Stock Exchange
K.S.E. Building
Stock Exchange Road
Off 1.1. Chundrigar Road
Karachi 74000, Pakistan
Phone: 92-21-111-001122/012345
Fax: 92-21-241-0825/5763/5136
Web site: http://www.kse.com.pk/

Lahore Stock Exchange
Stock Exchange Building
19 Khayaban-e-Aiwan-e-Iqbal
Lahore, Punjab 54000, Pakistan
Phone: 92-42-636-8000
Fax: 92-42-636-8484
Web site: http://www.lse.brain.net.pk/

Islamabad Stock Exchange
Stock Exchange Building
101-E, Fazal-UL-Haq Road
Blue Area, Islamabad, Pakistan
Phone: 92-51-215-047/50
Fax: 92-51-215-051

Philippines

Philippine Stock Exchange
Philippine Stock Exchange Centre
Exchange Road, Ortigas Center
Pasig, Metro Manila, Philippines
Phone: 63-2-636-0122/41
Fax: 63-2-634-5920
Web site: http://www.pse.com.ph/

Singapore

Stock Exchange of Singapore
20 Cecil Street
26-01/08 The Exchange
Singapore 049705
Phone: 65-535-3788
Fax: 65-535-2644
Web site: http://www.ses.com.sg/

Sri Lanka

Colombo Stock Exchange
#04-01, West Block
World Trade Center, Echelon Square
Colombo 1, Sri Lanka
Phone: 94-1-44-6581
Fax: 94-1-44-5279
Web site: http://lanka.com/stocks/cse/index.html

Taiwan (Republic of China)

Taiwan Stock Exchange
85 Yen Ping S. Road
Taipei, Taiwan
Phone: 886-2-311-4020
Fax: 886-2-311-4004
Web site: http://www.tse.com.tw/

Thailand

Stock Exchange of Thailand
132 Shindhorn Building Tower 1, 2nd Floor
Wireless Road
Bangkok 10330, Thailand
Phone: 66-2-254-0960
Fax: 66-2-254-3032
Web site: http://www.set.or.th/

Africa and Middle East Asia

Bahrain

Bahrain Stock Exchange
PO Box 3203
Bahrain
Phone: 973-24-3227
Fax: 973-27-6181

Botswana

Stockbrokers Botswana Ltd.
Ground Floor, Barclays House
Khama Crescent, PO Box 41015
Gaberone, Botswana
Phone: 267-357-900
Fax: 267-357-901

Egypt

Alexandria Stock Exchange
11 Talat Harb Street
Menshia
Alexandria, Arab Republic of Egypt
Phone: 20-3-483-5432

Egypt Stock Exchange
4-a, Elchrifeen Street
Cairo, Arab Republic of Egypt

Ghana

Ghana Stock Exchange
5th Floor, Cedi House
Liberia Road
Acca, Ghana
Phone: 233-21-669-908
Fax: 233-21-669-913

Iran

Tehran Stock Exchange
228, Hafez Avenue
Tehran 11389, Iran
Phone: 98-21-670-309
Fax: 98-21-672-524
Web site: http://www.neda.net/tse/

Israel

Tel Aviv Stock Exchange
54, Ahad Ha'am Street
Tel Aviv 65202, Israel
Phone: 972-3-567-7411
Fax: 972-3-510-5376
Web site: http://www.tase.co.il/

Ivory Coast (Cote d'Ivoire)

Abidjan Stock Exchange
Avenue Joseph Anoma
Immercible
Abidjan BVA01 BP, Ivory Coast
Phone: 225-215-742
Fax: 225-221-657

Jordan

Amman Financial Market
PO Box 8802
Amman, Jordan
Phone: 962-6-607-216
Fax: 962-6-686-830

Kenya

Nairobi Stock Exchange
1st Floor, Nation Centre
Kimathi Street, PO Box 43833
Nairobi, Kenya
Phone: 254-2-230-692
Fax: 254-2-224-200

Kuwait

Kuwait Stock Exchange
Web site: http://www.kuwait.net/~exchange/

Lebanon

Beirut Stock Exchange
Sadat Street
Sadat Tower, 2nd Floor
Beirut, Lebanon
Phone: 961-1-807-552
Fax: 961-1-807-331
Web site: http://www.lebanon.com/financial/stocks/index.htm

Malawi

Stockbrokers Ltd.- Malawi
Able House, Hannover Avenue
PO Box 358
Blantyre, Malawi
Phone: 265-621-817
Fax: 265-624-351

Malta

Malta Stock Exchange
27 Pietro Floriani Street
Floriana
Valletta 14, Malta
Phone: 356-244-051
Fax: 356-244-071

Mauritius

Stock Exchange of Mauritius
6th Floor, Les Cascades Building
33 Bis Edith Cavell Street
Port Louis, Mauritius
Phone: 230-212-9541/3
Fax: 230-208-8409

Morocco

Casablanca Stock Exchange
98, Boulevard Mohammed Vv
Casablanca, Morocco
Phone: 212-20-4110
Fax: 212-20-0365

Namibia

Namibian Stock Exchange
Ship 11, Kaiser Krone Centre
Post Street Mall
Windhoek, Namibia
Phone: 264-61-227-647
Fax: 264-61-248-531

Nigeria

Nagerian Stock Exchange
2/4 Custon Street
PO Box 2457
Lagos, Nigeria
Phone: 234-1-266-0287
Fax: 234-1-266-8724

Oman

Muscat Securities Market
Quaboos Mosque Street
MDB, Ruwi
Muscat 112, Oman
Phone: 968-702-607
Fax: 968-702-691

Palestine

Palestinian Securities Exchange
Web site: http://www.palnet.com/inv/bank2.htm

Saudi Arabia

Electronic Securities Information System
PO Box 2992
Riyadh 11169, Saudi Arabia
Phone: 966-1-466-2000
Fax: 966-1-463-3703

South Africa

Johannesburg Stock Exchange
17 Diagonal Street
PO Box 1174
Johannesburg 2000, South Africa
Phone: 27-11-377-2200
Fax: 27-11-834-7402
Web site: http://www.jse.co.za/welcome.htm

Swaziland

Swaziland Stockbrokers
2nd Floor, Dhlanudeka House, Walker St.
PO Box 2828
Mbabane, Swaziland
Phone: 268-46163
Fax: 268-44132

Tunisia

Tunis Stock Exchange
19 bis, rue Kamel Attaturk
Centre Babel Esc. E
Montplaisir 1002, Tunisia
Phone: 216-1-259-411
Fax: 216-1-347-256

Zambia

Lusaka Stock Exchange
Plot 2A, Cairo Road
Private Bag E731
Lusaka, Zambia
Phone: 260-1-228-391
Fax: 260-1-225-969

Zimbabwe

Zimbabwe Stock Exchange
8th Floor, Southampton House
Union Avenue, PO Box 1475
Harare, Zimbabwe
Phone: 263-4-727-907
Fax: 263-4-707-932